BUILDING UP
THE BODY OF
CHRIST

BUILDING UP
THE BODY OF
CHRIST

BRUCE M. HARTUNG

Published by Concordia Publishing House
3558 S. Jefferson Ave., St. Louis, MO 63118–3968
1-800-325-3040 • www.cph.org

Library of Congress Cataloging-in-Publication Data

Library of Congress Cataloging-in-Publication Data

Hartung, Bruce M.

Building up the body of Christ: skills for responsible church leadership / Bruce M. Hartung.

pages cm

Includes bibliographical references.

ISBN 978-0-7586-4442-8

1. Christian leadership. I. Title.

BV652.1.H273 2016

253--dc23

2015034500

1 2 3 4 5 6 7 8 9 10   25 24 23 22 21 20 19 18 17 16

Table of Contents

AS WE BEGIN

In the introduction to *Holding Up the Prophet's Hand: Supporting Church Workers,* I wrote that church workers "are called by God to apply the Gospel to the most daunting of human experiences. Is it any wonder that church workers sometimes succumb to dramatic risks of body, spirit, and self?"[1] I wrote that book hoping that lay leaders in congregations would read it. I still hope that.

Church professionals like pastors, teachers, deacons and deaconesses, directors of Christian education, directors of music, directors of Christian outreach, and lay ministers need intentional support from those they serve. But these church workers are not alone in being susceptible to these risks. The congregation's volunteer leaders, too, are subject to stress, conflict, interpersonal differences, and sin. Serving in the church opens people to real vulnerabilities, but church leaders can mobilize congregations in support of church workers. In fact, this support is part of what the followers of Christ are called to do for those among them who lead. In turn, church workers support and build up the whole community of Christ, the people of the congregation to which He has called them as servants. This dynamic goes both ways: church leaders need support from the congregation and the congregation needs support from its leaders.

---

1   Hartung, *Holding Up the Prophet's Hand,* 9.

I wrote *Building Up the Body of Christ: Supporting Community Life in the Church* as the follow-up to my earlier book for church professionals. The book takes its title from Ephesians 4:11–12:

> And He gave the apostles, the prophets, the evangelists, the shepherds and teachers, to equip the saints for the work of ministry, for building up of the body of Christ.

Life together in the local church, life in community, presents real vulnerabilities, and church leaders can mobilize to strengthen that community in tangible ways. Yet today's culture presents roadblocks. The cultural movement toward the individual and away from the community is well documented. Researcher and Harvard professor Robert Putnam was among the first to call attention to this trend in his article "Bowling Alone: America's Declining Social Capital," published in 1995.[2] Putnam reported on trends in bowling: there are many fewer bowling leagues in the United States today than there were several decades ago. Not only are we bowling alone, but most community service organizations are experiencing a decline in membership. In addition, the average age of those who belong to organizations like the Lions Club, the Elks Lodge, and the Veterans of Foreign Wars has risen markedly.

Putnam further studied this trend and, with Lewis Feldstein, published *Better Together: Restoring the American Community* in 2003. Efforts stimulated by Putnam's research findings continue in Harvard's Saguaro Seminar on Civic Engagement in America (www.hks.harvard.edu/programs/saguaro) to help citizens consider how social networks can be mobilized for civic good.

Congregations are not immune to this trend and are directly affected as participants in it. Church membership has declined. The "nones," people with no church affiliation, are now considered to be the second largest "religious" group in the nation, and congregations generally grow smaller as the average age of their membership rises. It would seem good, right, and salutary that we look more closely at the factors

---

2   Robert D. Putnam, "Bowling Alone: America's Declining Social Capital," *Journal of Democracy*, vol. 6, no. 1 (1995): 65–78.

that would strengthen our faith communities—that is, our congregations. This book provides basic tools to do that. Throughout *Building Up the Body of Christ*, the focus is on the characteristics, attitudes, and behaviors of congregation leadership. I use the term *church leaders* to refer to pastors, teachers, church council presidents, elders, deaconesses, and all other leadership roles. My goal is to help these leaders develop specific skills to build up the community, the Body of Christ, in the local church. More important than skill development is the development of the "person" of the church leader. Far too often, church leaders move too quickly to short-term techniques and quick fixes without assessing and strengthening themselves and others. Therefore, this book places considerable focus on the person of leaders, as well as their skills. For example, church leaders who effectively support congregational community begin with a secure sense of personal identity. They are immersed in the biblical understanding of leadership and church office; they see themselves as engaged in spiritual warfare; and they understand the challenges of burnout, stress, and even secondary traumatic stress. In short, they know who they are, they know what their vulnerabilities are, they know what their context is. Above all, they rely on their identity as baptized daughters and sons of God, made so by the life, death, and resurrection of Jesus Christ. Thus, they live empowered and blessed by the Holy Spirit.

Even so, church leaders need to develop specific characteristics and skills. They need to be trustworthy and responsive to others. They need to listen well. They need the ability to facilitate safe places, places where people can speak their minds and share the impulses of their hearts. Such leaders share openly, solicit regular feedback, and recognize the multiple influences that affect their capacity to lead. They understand how their own brains and the brains of others function, and they realize that brain function and environmental factors create differences among individuals, different personal styles and ways of doing things. They deal with differences and conflict creatively and welcome both as helpful in the processes of creative thinking and problem solving. This book focuses on these characteristics, attitudes, understandings, and skills.

To clarify these concepts and ideas, I have included many fictional short stories that show, in a practical way, how similar situations can be engaged and handled in any congregation. And where appropriate, I end most chapters with a few words of personal reflection and suggestions for additional reading on the topic of the chapter, a kind of take-the-next-step encouragement. I recommend these books and websites because I personally have found them to be immensely helpful in my own ministry. Like this book itself, all the resources I recommend have their flaws. Nevertheless, I believe they can be of benefit to you.

Of course, this book is not the only way that the life of a community, of a Christian congregation, might be addressed. Where this book is lacking, I hope others will fill the gap. And I hope that church leaders find my basic and focused approach helpful. In order for that to be so, I prayed that the Holy Spirit would bless the writing of this book. I also pray that He will bless its reading.

Over my many years as a pastoral counselor; as a denominational staff person concerned with the health, well-being, and life-long learning of church workers, their spouses, and their families; and as a teacher at a seminary, the people I spoke with taught me very much about life in general and, in particular, about life in the community. If I could list all those people who have influenced me and helped me write this book, I would likely exceed the pages I have available. Nevertheless, to all those folks who opened their lives to me in our conversations: thank you. I am deeply humbled and very grateful. This book would not have been written without you.

I want to thank specifically several people who made this book happen, either directly or indirectly.

More indirectly, Judy, my wife, is supportive and very patient with me. She does not like an overly messy space. We share desk space, and over the course of writing this book, my area became quite messy. Thanks, Judy, for your love, support, and care!

More directly, Pastor Chris Asbury and I have been in conversation over several years about spiritual warfare. He contributed a short essay about that in this book. Pastor Ethan Luhman also contributed a short essay on that same theme. Rev. Luhman offered invaluable help on the writing front. Debbie Roediger, my longtime administrative assistant, has been both patient and competent in helping me put this book into the format that Concordia Publishing House wants and needs. Thanks so much to all of you!

Finally, I wrote this book and, therefore, I am responsible for it. Any criticism or unhappiness with it should be addressed to me. If some readers will share their agreement and happiness with it, then that would be fine too. Most of all, though, my great desire is that church leaders find it useful and helpful, that the Body of Christ would indeed be built up, that Christ may be all and be in all, in our lives, congregations, and communities.

CHAPTER ONE

Considerations about Church Leaders and Their Leadership

The Bible has much to say about leadership. Whenever we talk about church leadership, we should begin there. God in Christ has a deep love for His Church, His people, and His leaders. So we expect nothing less than for Him to have words for us on how church leaders should lead.

St. Paul offers four major lists concerning the gifts of the Spirit and church leadership. I have included them below, together with some of their surrounding context. As you read them, look for themes and characteristics that emerge to guide us as we form a picture of the qualities necessary in such leadership.

> For by the grace given to me I say to everyone among you not to think of himself more highly than he ought to think, but to think with sober judgment, each according to the measure of faith that God has assigned. For as in one body we have many members, and the members do not all have the same function, so we, though many, are one body in Christ, and individually members one of another. Having gifts that differ according to the grace given to us, let us use

them: if prophecy, in proportion to our faith; if service, in our serving; the one who teaches, in his teaching; the one who exhorts, in his exhortation; the one who contributes, in generosity; the one who leads, with zeal; the one who does acts of mercy, with cheerfulness. (Romans 12:3–8)

Now concerning spiritual gifts, brothers, I do not want you to be uninformed. You know that when you were pagans you were led astray to mute idols, however you were led. Therefore I want you to understand that no one speaking in the Spirit of God ever says, "Jesus is accursed!" and no one can say "Jesus is Lord" except in the Holy Spirit.

Now there are varieties of gifts, but the same Spirit; and there are varieties of service, but the same Lord; and there are varieties of activities, but it is the same God who empowers them all in everyone. To each is given the manifestation of the Spirit for the common good. For to one is given through the Spirit the utterance of wisdom, and to another the utterance of knowledge according to the same Spirit, to another faith by the same Spirit, to another gifts of healing by the one Spirit, to another the working of miracles, to another prophecy, to another the ability to distinguish between spirits, to another various kinds of tongues, to another the interpretation of tongues. All these are empowered by one and the same Spirit, who apportions to each one individually as He wills. (1 Corinthians 12:1–11)

Now you are the body of Christ and individually members of it. And God has appointed in the church first apostles, second prophets, third teachers, then miracles, then gifts of healing, helping, administrating, and various kinds of tongues. Are all apostles? Are all prophets? Are all teachers? Do all work miracles? Do all possess gifts of healing? Do all speak with tongues? Do all interpret? But earnestly desire the higher gifts.

And I will show you a still more excellent way. If I speak in the tongues of men and of angels, but have not love, I am a noisy gong or a clanging cymbal. (1 Corinthians 12:27–13:1)

But grace was given to each one of us according to the measure of Christ's gift. . . . And He gave the apostles, the prophets, the evangelists, the shepherds and teachers, to equip the saints for the work of ministry, for building up the body of Christ, until we all attain to the unity of the faith and of the knowledge of the Son of God, to mature manhood, to the measure of the stature of the fullness of Christ, so that we may no longer be children, tossed to and fro by the waves and carried about by every wind of doctrine, by human cunning, by craftiness in deceitful schemes. Rather, speaking the truth in love, we are to grow up in every way into Him who is the head, into Christ, from whom the whole body, joined and held together by every joint with which it is equipped, when each part is working properly, makes the body grow so that it builds itself up in love. (Ephesians 4:7, 11–16)

St. Peter offers an additional look:

The end of all things is at hand; therefore be self-controlled and sober-minded for the sake of your prayers. Above all, keep loving one another earnestly, since love covers a multitude of sins. Show hospitality to one another without grumbling. As each has received a gift, use it to serve one another, as good stewards of God's varied grace: whoever speaks, as one who speaks oracles of God; whoever serves, as one who serves by the strength that God supplies—in order that in everything God may be glorified through Jesus Christ. To Him belong glory and dominion forever and ever. Amen. (1 Peter 4:7–11)

From these texts, several conclusions about church leaders, their leadership tasks, and the importance of spiritual gifts seem quite clear. These conclusions are interrelated, each influencing our understanding of the others. All of these passages have greatly influenced this book. I will draw from these throughout this text.

1. First, all offices in the church and all spiritual gifts are just that—gifts of the Spirit of God. Church leaders must see their personal spiritual gift or gifts in this way. While natural talents and abilities are clearly gifts from God, spiritual gifts and the offices we hold in the church also come to us as the work of the Holy Spirit, rather than as a result of our own efforts and abilities. Thus, instead of saying, "My strengths are . . . ," we more accurately say, "God has given me strengths in . . ."

   Scripture reveals that at times even St. Paul needed to be reminded of this. Note his discussion about his experience of weakness brought about by his thorn in the flesh, "a messenger of Satan":

   > So to keep me from becoming conceited because of the surpassing greatness of the revelations, a thorn was given me in the flesh, a messenger of Satan to harass me, to keep me from becoming conceited. Three times I pleaded with the Lord about this, that it should leave me. But He said to me, "My grace is sufficient for you, for My power is made perfect in weakness." Therefore I will boast all the more gladly of my weaknesses, so that the power of Christ may rest upon me. For the sake of Christ, then, I am content with weaknesses, insults, hardships, persecutions, and calamities. For when I am weak, then I am strong. (2 Corinthians 12:7–10)

   Paul also cautions us directly against the temptation to "think of [ourselves] more highly than [we] ought to think, but to think with sober judgment, each according to the measure of faith that God has assigned" (Romans 12:3).

   Spiritual gifts, and leadership in the church based on those gifts, are all "grace given to us" (Romans 12:6). It is God who "apportions to each one individually as He wills" (1 Corinthians 12:11). Spiritual gifts and offices are a "manifestation of the Spirit"

(1 Corinthians 12:7), not manifestations of the leader's own wisdom, insights, or efforts. Gifts are received, not humanly created. They are to be received with thanksgiving as gifts of God and used in the service of others (1 Peter 4:10).

2. The second conclusion we can draw from the writings of both Paul and Peter concerns the diversity of gifts and offices. Just as God gives different gifts, He also gives different leadership offices to different kinds of people. This is because such diversity of people, gifts, and offices is needed in the community of faith (1 Peter 4:9–11). The Holy Spirit distributes this marvelous diversity as He wills. This diversity is to be acknowledged and received by the community in thanksgiving because it is God's doing. There is no room in the Christian community for a hierarchical understanding of gifts that might say, "My gift of insight is greater than your gift of healing." Rather, there is a common "Praise God from whom all gifting comes, all of ours together."

3. The third insight is that one gift stands above all others and bathes them through and through: love. Even as we acknowledge all of God's other gifts and give thanks for them, love is common to all in the Christian community. Love is the gift that surrounds and the virtue that embraces all other gifts and offices. Immediately after Paul lists some of the offices and spiritual gifts God gives, he continues with the connecting phrase: "I will show you a still more excellent way" (1 Corinthians 12:31). Love infuses the other gifts and makes it possible for them to work in useful ways.

There is a challenging reality to this. If a gift or an office is used in a way that is not infused with love, it is but a noisy gong, a clanging cymbal (1 Corinthians 13:1). It creates dissonance. A good and useful thing becomes a problematic thing unless it is used within the context of love. It is possible, therefore, for any of God's gifts—wisdom, knowledge, healing, mighty deeds, and so on—to be used in darker ways. It is also possible for any of the individuals serving in the offices God gives—apostles, prophets, evangelists, pastors, and teachers—to behave in darker ways. This becomes a genuine concern and challenge. Rather than asking, "How good a prophet am I?" we should instead ask, "Am I fulfilling the duties of my office in a context of love?" Rather than asking, "How gifted is this person?" we should ask instead, "Is the leader behaving in a context of love?"

4. Finally, we can conclude from the Scriptures that spiritual gifts and churchly positions are not the end goal. They are not valued by either the gift itself or the office itself. Rather, they have a purpose and a goal beyond themselves, a greater end, which is "to equip the saints for the work of ministry, for building up the body of Christ" (Ephesians 4:12). God gives these gifts and offices for one purpose: to build up.

> Rather, speaking the truth in love, we are to grow up in every way into Him who is the head, into Christ, from whom the whole body, joined and held together by every joint with which it is equipped, when each part is working properly, makes the body grow so that it builds itself up in love. (Ephesians 4:15–16)

It is the building up of the community, of its members—Christ's Body, the Church—that is the point of it all. As that happens, everyone is stronger and more ready to do "the work of ministry" (Ephesians 4:12). Thus, no group of Christian people can ever boast, "Look how strong we have grown as a community, and we will keep getting stronger!" Rather, God's people focus on this: "By God's gracious gifts at work among us, we are growing stronger. He is building up our community so that we can do something—the work of ministry."

This is the central point about spiritual gifts and church offices: they are given for the common good, for the building up of the Body of Christ. (This is, of course, how this book gets its title.) God gives gifts not to glorify the individual or to extol the gifts themselves, but to glorify Christ and to build up the community that is called by His name. Therefore, God gives church leaders an office of leadership and the spiritual gifts they possess not because of their own inherent capacities and skills, but in grace and for the good of others. The Spirit gives many and diverse gifts, many offices, and many kinds of church leaders. He intends that all these be employed in the context of love. Love must infuse all spiritual gifts and church offices and, therefore, all church leaders.

God gives all spiritual gifts and all church offices for the building up of the community, which is the Body of Christ. Leaders who act in ways contrary to this fail to fulfill Paul's understanding of the faithful use of spiritual gifts and the faithful performance of church offices. On the other hand, leaders who understand themselves and see the gifts and offices of others in the light of these biblical truths will strive in the Spirit to strengthen those around them and be strengthened themselves as the Body of Christ is built up.

Carl and Katie were both longtime members of their congregation, and had served in many leadership positions. Currently, Carl chaired the board of elders and Katie was president of the board responsible for the congregation's early childhood school.

Each day as they prayed together, they always included a prayer of thanksgiving for the talents they had received from God and a petition that He teach them how to use those talents in constructive and helpful ways.

Together they regularly took counsel with their pastor. Once a month, they participated with other church leaders who met to discuss books about the Christian life, church leadership, or Bible exposition. Additionally, they belonged to a small group of other couples that met monthly for Bible study. In the groups they led, Carl and Katie both scheduled regular feedback sessions that specifically focused on how their leadership was being received.

Life was exceptionally good for Katie and Carl. They were admired and respected by practically everyone in the congregation and were extremely valued as capable church leaders by their ministerial staff.

Warning! C. F. W. Walther, founder of The Lutheran Church— Missouri Synod, includes the following thesis in his book *The Proper*

Distinction Between Law and Gospel: "[T]he Word of God is not rightly divided when a description is given of faith, both as regards its strength and the consciousness and productiveness of it, that does not fit all believers at all times."[3] As he comments on this thesis, Walther reflects on Paul's experience: "For I know that nothing good dwells in me, that is, in my flesh. For I have the desire to do what is right, but not the ability to carry it out" (Romans 7:18):

> The true Christian, he says, always desires what is good, but frequently does not accomplish it. Now, then, if a preacher describes a Christian in such a manner as to deny that, unless he accomplishes all that is good, he does not really will what is good, the description is unbiblical. Frequently he does not progress beyond the good will to do something. Before he is aware of it, he has gone astray; the sin within him has come forth, and he is ashamed of himself. But for that reason he has not by any means fallen from grace.[4]

The picture of Carl and Katie in its close-to-perfect form painted above is impossible. In this fallen and sinful world, all people, including church leaders, truly do miss the mark. We miss it often! In one way or another, church leaders fall short of perfection. Painting a picture of perfect church leaders as though this were reality is always a "preaching of the Law," to use Walther's terminology. Such an ideal state is not obtainable in this life.

If, however, the picture is painted as one toward which we imperfectly strive, then it is a different matter. And if in the painting of such a picture, the cross and resurrection of Jesus Christ and the gifting of the Holy Spirit are front and center, then it can help church leaders grow toward a Spirit-driven goal. Even then we must remember that our imperfections will always draw us back to the grace, love, and forgiveness of Jesus as we grow imperfectly. Confessing, forgiven, loved, and Spirit-empowered, we grow, and in our growth, we are better able to lead as God's people, called to build up the Body of Christ so that the work of

---

3   Walther, *The Proper Distinction Between Law and Gospel*, 3.

4   Walther, *The Proper Distinction Between Law and Gospel*, 308–9.

ministry goes on apace.

In 1932, J. H. C. Fritz, academic dean of Concordia Seminary, painted a picture of a church leader, specifically that of a pastor. Yet we can apply his words to all church leaders: "The words of an older writer still hold true, that 'a holy pastor has but three books to study—the Scriptures, himself, and his flock.'"[5]

For church leaders, our "study" is an ongoing enterprise. Our study is never done; our task is never finished—on this side of heaven. Church leaders continue to study the Bible. We continue to study ourselves to become more self-aware. And we continue to learn to know people (that is, the flock). All three areas of study are essential.

In some places, Fritz's text reads as if it was greatly influenced by the psychology and sociology of his time. He leads readers into a more holistic view of study; for example, one that takes up the wisdom God has made available in the behavioral sciences. But his use of these sciences is always subservient to theology and always purposeful. Fritz intends to help church leaders better understand both themselves and others so they can be better leaders, so they more ably "equip the saints for the work of ministry, for building up the body of Christ" (Ephesians 4:12).

All of this study of Scripture, of self, and of others is done imperfectly. People who study never know it all—and they know that! Church leaders do not know everything about Scripture, themselves, or others. We make mistakes; we damage relationships; our inadequate knowledge and impure motives bring trouble. But we recognize that everyone who lives in the Body of Christ lives as both a saint and a sinner, adequate and inadequate, knowledgeable and educate-able. In a real sense, church leaders understand, in the very core of their being, that as forgiven and redeemed followers of Christ in a fallen and imperfect world, they are continuous learners. Learning for church leaders becomes, as Peter Vaill says in the title of his book, "learning as a way of being."

Because of this understanding, church leaders seek the help, support, and wisdom of others. As learners, they see themselves as people who

---

5   Fritz, *Pastoral Theology*, 8.

are growing to be better able to "equip the saints for the work of ministry, for building up the body of Christ" (Ephesians 4:12). This is the essential nature of a learning and growing community, a picture toward which all imperfect, forgiven, and Spirit-driven church leaders strive.

Speaking Personally

In my own life and spiritual journey, I have wrestled with the experience Walther writes about. I have in mind a picture of who and what I should be like as a child of God. The picture is prefaced by an important preposition: "If I am a Christian, then I will . . . " Each time I fail to live up to my ideal, I'm tempted to question whether I am a "real Christian," a "strong-enough Christian." This is the very essence of my vulnerability in spiritual warfare. (Perhaps it is yours as well.) Satan asks, "Bruce, since you obviously do not live up to your own ideal, are you sure you are a worthy leader or even a true Christian? Really?"

This question points me in the wrong direction! I am a child of God totally because of God's action for me in Christ. I am a Christian because of Christ and what He did for me on the cross. I strive to imitate my Savior. But in this life, as the Holy Spirit empowers me, I will always be on the road, moving toward that ideal. I will arrive at that destination only in eternity.

As you take up this book, it is essential for you to remember that. Nothing I suggest here can be perfectly achieved. Each of us is striving toward the ideal. None of us has yet arrived. Please, therefore, consider the ideals here as beckoning you forward toward learning and growth, not as a goal that will be perfectly attained in this life.

J. H. C. Fritz's *Pastoral Theology* has been a very important book for me. Given when it was written, parts of it seem quite prescient. I recommend that you read it.

I also recommend that you meditate on Romans 12; 1 Corinthians 12–13; Ephesians 4; and 1 Peter 4.

Finally, consider reading Peter Vaill's book *Learning As a Way of Being: Strategies for Survival in a World of Permanent White Water.*

Spiritual Warfare

Diablos 6755: This is Diablos 6755 reporting on the DNN (Devil's News Network) from the millennial gathering of returning warriors from the field. With me is Diablos 8964, who has been in the fight on earth for the last one hundred years. So, 8964, you look healthy and well for all you have been through. What is your secret?

Diablos 8964: Actually, it is pretty simple once you get the hang of it. We haven't fooled around much with those on the outside. We take on the top insiders—leaders in their churches—elders, presidents, lay leaders, school principals, directors of Christian education, and pastors, among many, many other kinds of humans. We target everybody who provides leadership to others of their kind. We work to deceive them and then bring them down.

Diablos 6755: Let us in on your trade secrets (but don't give too much away since we can't tell who hacks into our secure network).

Diablos 8964: Sure. First, we research their lives and find their vulnerabilities. We don't create anything, since we have to have God's permission to do that, like He gave to our leader in Job's case. So, all we have to do is to simply find out where their weaknesses are, and we begin there.

Diablos 6755: Sounds very effective. Time is short, but can you give us an example?

Diablos 8964: Say one of their leaders has grown up in a family in which he felt he was never good enough to merit his parents' unconditional love. He's got that inside of him. Basically his inner question is, "Am I good enough?" Then, whenever something happens that doesn't go well, he says to himself, "Well, that proves that I am no good," and he begins to despair. If we can grab hold of that despair and isolate him from others so he is alone with his despair, then we are on our way. Despair is a toehold. Isolation from others and their support and help is where we get a real foothold. All kinds of things happen then. He falls, takes others with him, and it's just wonderful. We get the leader and a few others in this trap. This has worked really well. Notice, I just have a few little scratches after a hundred years.

Diablos 6755: Thanks, 8964. Here comes another fighter. He looks a bit more wounded. Let's find out what he's been up to. Welcome! You are?

Diablos 10769: I am Diablos 10769, and am I glad to see friendly faces. It's hell out there.

Diablos 6755: Tell us about it. Looks like and sounds like things have not been easy for you.

Diablos 10769: Seeking Christians to devour is hard work. The first problem is when they recognize me. When I am hidden and they are not looking for spiritual factors, they are easier prey. But when they see who I am and when they have others around them who help and support them, I am in real trouble. I call in reinforcements, but together they have the power—it's almost like God's very power—to fend me off. Then they attack me. Can you imagine that? I have often had to run for my life.

Diablos 6755: How do they attack?

Diablos 10769: Well, they gather in large and small groups for strategy and planning that comes when they read from the Book. They come together to share what their temptations are, and some of them even go to their—what do they call them . . . "pastors"?—to actually confess them. Can you imagine? What's really hurtful is that they sing stuff together. Sometimes just as they are walking along, like this tune "Lift High the Cross." So discouraging. And worst of all, they consume the very body and blood of the name that shall never be on my lips.

Diablos 6755: Sounds like a tough fight.

Diablos 10769: You've got that right. Every once in a while, I get a toehold with one of them, but then that one goes and talks with his friends, and I can't keep hold of the toe. Excuse me, I've got to get to the Evil Growth Center to learn some new ways to get at being more of a roaring lion.

Diablos 6755: Good luck, 10769. Diablos 12841, can you give us just a moment?

Diablos 12841: Yes! But I am in a hurry.

Diablos 6755: You look in fine shape. What was your key to fighting well?

Diablos 12841: Damage their relationships! Help them find lots of things they dislike in each other, and then magnify those dislikes.

Diablos 6755: How do you do that?

Diablos 12841: Put in their hearts that they are really not together, that their differences are personal and that they are alone. Got to run! I am late for my workshop on how to create even deeper and better divisions between people—make them dislike each other by pretending they really love each other. This will be great fun.

Diablos 6755: We've got just a minute or two. Let's see who we can . . . oh, there is Diablos 5. Diablos 5, can we have a quick word with you?

Diablos 5: Absolutely.

Diablos 6755: Can you tell us truthfully how the warfare goes?

Diablos 5: Truthfully, the war is over. But the battle rages on, and, who knows, maybe we can make a difference. We can tempt and divide and discourage and deceive and divert. And we will continue to do that until the end comes, whenever that will be. We will mess up lives, we will cause havoc, we will break up communities. Sometimes we will succeed. Our best success comes when we are not recognized. Our best shot at not being recognized is in the more, shall we say, sophisticated world, where all explanations are made in a natural, physical, what-they-can-see way. In a sophisticated world like that, no one looks for the spiritual. No one sees us. That's when we do well!

Diablos 6755: Thank you very much, esteemed 5. Wise words from a wise leader. Diablos 6755 reporting for DNN as warriors return after a millennium. May their time here be refreshing and may their continuing education at the Evil Growth Center bring increasing knowledge and rich rewards. Now, back to you in the studio.

"Be sober-minded; be watchful. Your adversary the devil prowls around like a roaring lion, seeking someone to devour" (1 Peter 5:8).

Church leaders always see the world as a spiritual battlefield, although, of course, that is not the only way to see the world. Basically, in a worldview that is holistic and not divided into independent compartments, spiritual life and warfare are not in a single compartment where they have no particular influence on other parts of a person's life. Rather, the spiritual is integrated throughout all of life. There is no such thing as a totally secular happening. The physical and the spiritual are intertwined in the lives of all people and cannot be separated. All of life has a spiritual-life-and-warfare component, including more positive questions such as "What will the Holy Spirit teach us as we walk through life's joys and difficulties?"

Church leaders who see the world in this way recognize their need to be armed with the weaponry that strengthens them in battle. But spiritual warfare is not all defensive. It is also offensive, as when it is used to actively break down the gates of hell.

Church leaders understand and believe that the weaponry is God's revealed Word and the blessed Sacraments that are the Means of God's Grace. But the weaponry also includes the community that is the Body of Christ, where Christians are fed, supported, encouraged, protected, challenged, and loved.

Church leaders know that much spiritual warfare goes on in the hearts and minds of the leaders themselves and in the hearts and minds of all followers of Christ as war is waged against the world, the devil, and their flesh.

Church leaders recognize that Satan's primary tactic is to exploit the vulnerability of the follower of Christ and the community of believers. That is why church leaders need not only to be built up, but also to be led in a way that builds up the Body of Christ.

Here are some of the dynamics of spiritual warfare, courtesy of the sparrow trap, which is a picture of spiritual warfare: temptation, action, entrapment, and believing there is no way out (even though there actually is).

Sparrow Trap Features: It has two holding compartments. The first or main lobby is accessible by 2 "funnel" doors. The second compartment can only be entered by passing through another funnel door which leads from inside the main lobby. These funnel doors work by allowing target sparrows to "squeeze" in comfortably but when they attempt to reverse their path and try to leave they find the funnel uncomfortable. Rather than risk hurting them-selves, most will choose to simply stay in the trap.

These entrances are adjustable so if needed you can make them smaller or larger. This ability to adjust the funnel opening enables the trapper to then target sparrows of two sizes or even different species.[6]

The features of this sparrow trap include bait (temptation), positive response to the bait (action), awareness of being confined (entrapment), and assumption that resistance is futile (no way out). In fact, there is a way out, but anxiety and work, challenge, and discomfort are connected with escape.

In spiritual warfare, the bait is sometimes external and sometimes internal. But the Christian must respond to the bait for temptation to work. Job teaches us that it is possible for God to give Satan permission to cause misfortune. However, generally, the evil that already exists is quite enough. The bait already exists inside the individual, in the world, and from Satan or, in more classical formulations, the world, the flesh, and the devil. The task of all the demons on the planet is to exploit what already exists in the world and in the individual believer.

When church leaders look through the lens of spiritual warfare, they see that many challenges are embedded and that these challenges may weaken the congregation's and each individual's witness to Jesus. It is likely also true that as an individual or a congregation becomes more

---

6   "Bird Traps," Bugspray.com, accessed July 29, 2015, www.bugspraycart.com/traps/cage/starlingsparrow-10-x-16-x-24.HTML. In a private communication discussing permission to use this picture and text, Jonathan, of U-Spray, Inc. wrote: "I can see a sequence of 'en-trapment' this trap uses, which can resemble the decisions we make in life. Not sure if it's the one you're referencing but it's very clear to me how one bad decision can lead you down a 'one-way road.' This one-way road may look innocent enough when you first get on the path, but inevitably, things will get progressively worse. Now, does one have to 'go with the flow' of traffic and just continue in the same direction without fighting the flow of the tide? No. They can go against the tide, fight the path, and as hard as might be, turn their life around and exit the 'trap.' It may seem daunting, and clearly it won't be the easiest path to follow. But it will be paramount for the individual if they want to lead a happy, fulfilled, and balanced life."

active in their communities and in outreach, they will come under more and more attack.

Spiritual warfare has strategies that can be discerned. Spiritual director Jane Guenther suggests the following simple process of spiritual attack: gaining a toehold, gaining a foothold, and gaining a stronghold.[7] Spiritual warfare is an ongoing process that has the capacity to increase in intensity and strength. Louis Cameli suggests that the ordinary work of the devil is deception, division, diversion, and discouragement.[8] Ed Murphy proposes that Satan's operation is a strategy of deception, the target being the leaders, with the end goal of dishonoring God through the fallen leaders.[9]

What can be exploited in the lives of individual believers and, therefore, church leaders? Just about anything! The questions, then, for church leaders are these: In what ways can Satan exploit, or try to exploit, me? In what ways can Satan exploit our congregation and our community?

A useful exercise for church leaders in relation to these aspects of spiritual warfare is to have a personal reckoning—through meditation, prayer, or journaling or writing—of areas of vulnerability to spiritual exploitation by the demons who walk about. Once the areas of vulnerability to satanic strategies have been identified, the church leader should consult with a spiritual director, mature Christian leader, pastor (or fellow pastor), or pastoral counselor to begin to work on addressing those areas.

Another useful effort is to use the same exercise in a group to explore the group's areas of vulnerability to spiritual exploitation. After considering the nature of spiritual warfare, members of the group share their ideas about the group's vulnerability. Once the list of satanic strategies has been developed, use some of the group's meeting time to begin to work, prayerfully, on addressing those areas. Looking through the lens of spiritual warfare in a group context means, for instance, that group

---

7   Jane Guenther, private conversation.
8   Cameli, *The Devil You Don't Know.*
9   Murphy, *The Handbook for Spiritual Warfare:* Revised and Updated, 19–20.

members who have unfinished angry business with one another are not just harboring interpersonal conflicts to be settled by totally secular means. It means there is also a conflict with a spiritual component, which creates barriers to both the building up of the Body of Christ and the group's capacity to serve.

In the midst of this, church leaders retain a sense of self-challenge and humility. Remembering that even the great apostle St. Peter was, in at least one instance, unknowingly an agent of Satan (Matthew 16:21–23), all leaders know that without the Holy Spirit working in their self-reflection and awareness, they may join Peter as an unknowing agent of Satan. This is why the spiritual walk in the midst of spiritual warfare is not solitary, but is taken with other members of the Body of Christ. This community provides the opportunity for discernment and feedback.

It is also helpful for church leaders to remember that they have a certain oneness with St. Paul when he shares his own spiritual ambiguity of wanting to do good but ending up doing evil and of being at war with himself. This ambiguity and experience forces him to turn to the only one who can provide deliverance: Jesus (Romans 7:14–25).

Church leaders thus recognize that they are not engaged in spiritual warfare by themselves. In warfare, church leaders turn to Jesus, who fights with them and for them and, indeed, has already claimed the victory. "Though devils all the world should fill, All eager to devour us, We tremble not, we fear no ill; They shall not overpow'r us. This world's prince may still Scowl fierce as he will, He can harm us none. He's judged; the deed is done; One little word can fell him" (*LSB* 656:3).

Church leaders also recognize that others in the community of believers are alongside them in spiritual warfare.

> "The spiritual journey is not to be a solitary walk but a community pilgrimage." The isolated, self-guiding ascetic is vulnerable to spiritual imbalance. Balanced spiritual formation is cultivated in the company of like-minded comrades and sensitive confidants. We draw wisdom and comfort from one another; we encourage and are encouraged by the example of our fellow Christians. To pursue

spirituality alone is folly, and ultimately it misses the point of being the body of Christ.[10]

Church leaders understand that obstacles to life in the community include disconnectedness and individualism. As solo characters, church leaders (and all individuals within the church community) will be more and more vulnerable to spiritual warfare exploitation. "We share our mutual woes, Our mutual burdens bear, And often for each other flows The sympathizing tear" (*LSB* 649:3) is not possible if church leaders and members are disconnected or see themselves as on a solitary walk. Among the functions of the community are support, accountability, growth, building up, and discernment.

As I suggested in another place:

> We are connected to one another in the Christian community not simply by the bonds of human relationships and good will, not simply by the bonds of emotion and personal experience, but fundamentally, we are joined together in and through Christ. We celebrate the gifts Christ gives each of us for the good of all of us, and we work to help one another enhance and grow the gifts Christ has given.[11]

Jim was twenty-four years old and Liz was twenty-three. They had been dating for about a year and a half and engaged for a month. In the last six months, a sexual relationship had begun to be more and more tempting. Something had changed, or at least was changing, in their relationship as they discussed the question of how far they would go sexually. They had not had intercourse, but both were concerned that it was getting close to happening. They were also aware that more and more of their conversation turned to this concern.

Both were active in their congregation, and so they decided to go to Pastor George to discuss this. "I am really bothered by this," Jim said. "Our relationship was not born out of sex, but out of becoming really

---

10 Gordon Johnston, "Old Testament Community and Spiritual Formation" in *Foundations of Spiritual Formation: A Community Approach to Becoming Like Christ*, 78.

11 Hartung, *Holding Up the Prophet's Hand*, 59.

good friends. We both decided that we would hold off having a sexual relationship until we were married. But . . ."

"We are struggling with this," Liz broke in. "It is like this is most of what we talk about these days. Something is different."

As the conversation progressed, it became clear to Pastor George that Liz and Jim were struggling with this in almost desperate ways. After exploring this for a while, and after learning that they wanted him to help them with this, he asked a question: "Liz, Jim, think about what has changed in your lives in the past six months besides this."

"Really not much, Pastor," said Liz. "We both have our same jobs and same friends, and life is generally good, except for this."

"The only thing that I can think of," Jim shared, "is that I took the volunteer position here as one of the adult heads of the youth program. I share that with Noah."

"And," Pastor George wondered, "what effect would the two of you having sex have on your work with the youth?"

Jim looked both stunned and puzzled. "Honestly, Pastor George, I think I would resign my post. I would not feel right about leading the youth if I was having intercourse with Liz."

"Do you think that may have something to do with this?" Pastor George continued.

"Hmm," both Liz and Jim said almost in unison.

Liz and Jim were targets of Diablos 10769.

As the three of them discussed how Liz and Jim were involved in spiritual warfare in this way, they decided to pray together. The couple decided to read devotional materials for engaged couples every day, as well. They committed to continue to talk with Pastor George and to participate every week in the Divine Service of Sacrament and Word.

No wonder Diablos 10769 returned to the millennial gathering wounded.

While the temptations remained because Jim and Liz were physically attracted to each other, the obsession with the sexual issues diminished and, seven months later, they married.

No amount of continuing education at the Evil Growth Center would give Diablos 10769 power to exploit Jim and Liz. As Diablos 10769 said, "They come together to share what their temptations are, and some of them even go to their—what do they call them . . . "pastors"?—to actually confess them. Can you imagine?"

Speaking Personally

Chapters like this are hard for me to write. I am highly influenced by naturalistic explanations that focus on the physical—on what can be seen and, therefore, explained in terms of nature or science. This is a knee-jerk response to what I see in myself, in others, and in the world. I see people struggling with life issues that are, on the one hand, understandable without using a spiritual lens. I see myself struggling with such issues as well, of course. But when I put on the glasses of spiritual warfare, I see a very different world. I see a world where the scientifically explained struggle has church leadership implications. I have seen the struggles of church leaders become magnified and eventually become public in such a way that their positions are compromised, and sometimes even destroyed. The talents and usefulness of a church leader to build up the Body of Christ are reduced or even lost and, thus, the Body is less built up or, worse, injured.

In my own struggle, I see the demonic attack directly. For example, I have lost track of how many times I have had the impulse to remove this chapter from the book. Another example is the thought that I should not write the book at all, since I am but a beggar before God. When my struggle gets more intense, my thoughts go darker: since I struggle, should I even be teaching or speaking? And the ultimate question: since I struggle, am I still saved?

Here is the satanic-caused confusion that equates being in a spiritual struggle with being good enough (or having enough good works) to be saved. Jesus saves! My struggle and yours is one of living a life in Christ and also in this world.

I need others around me who will help me keep looking through the lens. I need others who will help me not become so paranoid that I see demons under every rock. So I talk about and write about spiritual warfare that I might be reminded and, perhaps, others will be reminded as well. I am comforted that Jesus fights for me and with me in this battle and, indeed, is already victorious on my behalf.

There is a great deal of writing about spiritual warfare outside of the Lutheran Church that should be approached with a reflective and discerning mind. Even so, there is much value to the works from diverse perspectives. Two books I have found particularly helpful are Karl Payne's *Spiritual Warfare: Christians, Demonization, and Deliverance* and Louis Cameli's *The Devil You Don't Know: Recognizing and Resisting Evil in Everyday Life.* I think it most helpful when several people read these books at the same time and gather together to discuss them. As I mentioned in the introduction, I will be suggesting next-step readings that I have found to be particularly useful. As in all things human, the readings are not perfect, but I think they can be helpful.

CHAPTER THREE

Four Challenges to Church Leaders

In *Holding Up the Prophet's Hand*, I suggested that there are four major challenges for church workers: spiritual warfare, burnout, stress, and secondary traumatic stress. That these are challenges for church leaders is especially true, but church workers and lay leaders of all kinds also experience them. This chapter will provide a brief summary of these four challenges.

SPIRITUAL WARFARE

Spiritual warfare was discussed in the previous chapter. Here, John Kleinig, an Australian Lutheran theologian, can be additionally and essentially helpful. He writes (I substituted some words, indicated by brackets):

> If we heed what Luther has to say about the role of the devil in the spiritual formation of [church leaders], we will realize our [congregations and other church organizations and communities] are spiritual battlegrounds, contested places, rather than spiritual oases, places of refuge from temptation. We will also be able to help our [church leaders] understand why they and their families come under such concerted attack at certain points during their [time

of leadership in the congregation and other church organizations and communities].[12]

Church leaders and church workers are especially vulnerable to spiritual warfare. Two pastors comment on this reality. Chris Asbury, a Lutheran Church—Missouri Synod pastor, writes concerning spiritual warfare as he has seen it in parish life:

> I see warfare daily in ministry. Members lose sight of the cross; Jesus continues to hold it before us. People doubt; Jesus remains faithful. Young and old openly sin; Jesus freely forgives. We hurt one another, thinking we are right; Jesus heals and makes right. We replace the Gospel with good works, politics, and personal agendas; Jesus' Word continues to accomplish that for which it is sent. My prayers lack zeal; Jesus prays for me. My efforts prove futile, assumptions steer incorrectly, successes even turn to failure; God's plans prevail anyway. What's going on in these situations?
>
> Satan still wages war against our Creator and His creatures. Man felt this painfully first in Genesis 3; Adam, once tempted, fell dead. John 1 and 3 show the effect this brought on all creation, especially humanity. Romans 3 agrees with our plight: though we were made to reflect God's clear image of love and glory to the world, all have fallen short; we resemble shattered mirrors. Satan, however, is never greater or stronger than the Lord. Evil exhausts and numbs our weak flesh, but Jesus took on all flesh. He died, and rose, and God restores His image in us through Jesus' victory over the evil one (in the wilderness, at Golgotha, and through the empty garden tomb).
>
> All my relationships daily experience lack of love for neighbor and hatred of God grown from seeds of doubt. We see—sometimes more clearly than others—Satan, the

---

12 Kleinig, *Grace Upon Grace: Spirituality for Today*, 16.

world, and our flesh teaming up to drag down and devour us, leaders and laymen alike. How they team against us confounds us in mystery, yet we readily, sinfully, suffer this exploitation instead of fearing, loving, and trusting in God above all things. Doubt, disobedience, hatred, licentiousness, lies, gossip, and discontentment are the evils I see most in myself, my congregation, community, and world. Leaders provide greater targets.

Christ is the only way out of this living hell. Regardless of our emotions and experience, Christ reigns as King by the Gospel. He gives us His Holy Spirit to deliver His gifts to us, thereby delivering us from the evil one and all evil. Even as God re-birthed us by Baptism once and for all time, He also makes us holy by daily killing and raising us in Christ. Although our experience with evil continues east of Eden awaiting the new paradise, the Holy Spirit works in us (Christ's new creation) that which is pleasing, until the eschatological Day He completes His work; Jesus freely forgives and teaches us to obey all He commands, making us bear fruit in keeping with repentance. This is the Holy Spirit's sanctifying work.

Our efforts fail when we rely on human strength to resist Satan's three-headed monster. Just as we cannot by our own reason or strength believe in Jesus Christ, but rely on the Holy Spirit to give us faith, so we must rely on the Holy Spirit to sanctify and keep us in the true faith by the power of God's Word and sacramental gifts.

For me, Luther's Small Catechism has proved invaluable in life and ministry. Luther explains that our warfare is all about the Word: ears to hear it and hearts to obey it. But our fleshly ears deafen themselves to the Word and our hearts disobey God. Jesus gives us prayer to confess our sins and seek the King in His Gospel kingdom. In the first, second, and third petitions, especially, God's Word proves to be central to our faith life; look there in the Small Catechism and ask, if we take God's Word away what do we get?

All of my relationships can grow more fruit in purity, fidelity, and love. Whether with leader or layman, our relationships have not yet attained perfection, so Christ saves and the Holy Spirit sanctifies. In what specific ways do you currently see this need? How have you at times deafened your ears or disobeyed God's Word? How has the Word already saved and sanctified you?

Ephesians 6 shows us all the armor Christ provides to defend us as He guards and guides us in everyday relationships (see also Ephesians 5). With each piece of armor, Christ—who is strong—provides specific protection for us—who are weak; head to toe, Jesus covers us entirely with Himself.

Evil is obvious (plastered in our nightly news, memories, and Facebook feeds), but our subtle evil in life and ministry is perhaps more devious and destructive; for, by subtle, silent evil we permit Satan to gain toeholds, footholds, and immense control of our lives and we unwittingly boil like frogs in a pot as the temperature is gradually raised. Thankfully, Scripture and our Lutheran Confessions give us Jesus; they help us see evil in us and around us, feel creation's pain and hear more clearly her groaning, but also provide healing: Christ for us, all people, even all creation.

Ethan Luhman, also an LCMS pastor, writes as a 2015 graduate of Concordia Seminary, St. Louis, as he saw spiritual warfare in his seminary experience:

You'd think that the seminary would be an easy place to be a great Christian. In my experience, however, it was anything but. The seminary resembled more of a battleground than a peaceful place with the light from above shining down. To come to the seminary means to leave the community one naturally lives in, and thus, to leave behind most every meaningful relationship one has. Personally, I struggled with loneliness. I struggled with being open and honest in this new community. Can people be trusted? Are they looking out for me? Am I good enough to meet their standards of what a pastor should be? I found myself dwelling on my insecurities, on past sins, on all the things that were wrong with me. This also made it easier to dwell on all the things that were wrong with everyone else.

How should we define ourselves? Clearly by what Christ has done. But Satan's greatest trick is to convince us that we are defined by all the things we have done. My issues with others should not be seen as ways to put the blame on others, but rather as opportunities to build them up. My frustration was focused falsely on the wrong people. I had become caught up in dwelling on defects.

But isn't that just what evil would want? Here I am, at a place where people are gathered to follow Jesus, and I am missing out on the beauty of the Body of Christ in this place. I am missing out on my own personal beauty—made in the image of God, restored by Jesus, dwelling place of the Holy Spirit. There is a spirit who is driven mad by this reality, Satan, and he did his best to help me see the worst—in myself and in others, but most importantly, in the Body of Christ. And at times, I fell prey to Satan's attacks. The more and more I became aware of the work he was up to at the seminary, and in my personal life, the more I could guard against it.

I don't want to blame all my struggles on spiritual warfare. In fact, I don't think I could honestly separate it out and say, "This was the work of Satan. This was my foolishness. This was that guy's fault." I am responsible for evil, and so is almost every part of the not-quite-yet-perfect Body of Christ. But I am not going to let that blind me from the reality that there is evil at work in the world, separate from the will of man. Will I be one with the Holy Spirit (and the whole Body of Christ), or one with evil spirits? Will I be quick to say, "Look what Jesus is doing!" or will I be quick to say, "Look what *you* are doing!"?

I know Jesus is at work when I see even the worst of situations as opportunities to build up His Body, and I know evil is at work when I see even the best of situations as opportunities to tear down and separate myself and others from the Body of Christ. As I leave the seminary, I know the warfare will continue and even become heightened, and my prayer is that I continue to dwell in the unity I have with all believers—and with Jesus Himself—through the Holy Spirit He has given to us, and that all other spirits may be kept far away from the beautiful Body of Jesus Christ in this place.

In transparency and honesty, and by their own examples, Asbury and Luhman encourage church leaders to engage in conversation about spiritual warfare and to look through the lens of spiritual warfare at their lives, their ministries, and the communities of which they are a part.

BURNOUT

Many church leaders, especially as they begin their service to the congregation, take up their task with hope and vision. While there are many reasons for becoming a church leader, the desire to lead, to make a difference, is active through the Holy Spirit in the heart of church leaders. Wanting to make a difference and contribute to the health and well-being of congregation and even denomination life, they agree to accept election or appointment to a position of leadership.

When the initial capacity to make a difference runs up against realities in the congregation that interfere with that church leader's hope and vision, burnout slowly rears its head.

Micah was a take-charge character. Full of energy and brimming with ideas, he impressed many with his zeal and was elected the president of his congregation after being a member for only four years.

Most of the congregation's leadership was considerably older than Micah.

Micah and his business partner, Rex, had founded a real estate company seven years before that had grown from a two-person operation to one with six sales and two administrative support staff. Part of the success of their business was the high-energy, fast-acting, assertive style that both Micah and Rex had. As business owners, both had utilized their capacity to attract the best people to the company.

One year after becoming president of his congregation, Micah was talking with Rex over coffee. "I love our church, but everything moves too slowly, so much so that I can't get done what I want to get done," lamented Micah.

"It's a different railroad to run, that's for sure," Rex reflected.

"Frankly, I'm thinking of stepping down at the end of my two-year term," Micah said. "I had lots of energy to get things done right away. We need a fund-raising campaign for a bigger parking lot, and we need more outreach to the community, and we need shorter church services, all to attract more people. But I can't get any of that done. People are slow to change and even slower to adopt my direction. And worse, I'm not as enthusiastic as I was when I was elected. I think my love of our church is turning to frustration and cynicism."

Micah was on fire when he became the president; that fire is growing less and less intense. Burnout happens when the fire is barely alive or even goes out. It has been said that in order to burn out, one must have been on fire at one time. Micah was more vulnerable to burnout because he had energy and passion. He entered his church position with hope and vision, but he was frustrated by the realities of his congregation, combined with his own intensity.

The word *burnout* is often used generically to describe any situation in which a person grows tired, lacking energy and passion for the vocation he or she is doing. This more general use of the word sometimes obscures the more specific reality of burnout: the vision and hope that church leaders have to be helpful and influential in what they consider to be important and vital directions for a congregation has run into barriers, roadblocks, realities, and even resistance. When this happens, church leaders can lose enthusiasm for the very things that had motivated them to enter into leadership in the first place.

Burnout happens when a new teacher enters a classroom hoping that students will capture his or her excitement for learning, but then discovers that many do not. It happens when a director of Christian education begins a new ministry with the hope of doubling the size of the youth group, but then those numbers don't rise. It happens when the new chairman of the board of elders wants all elders to make personal contact with the church families assigned to them, and the other elders move slowly or not at all. It happens when a new men's group chairman believes the group can be revitalized and, two years into his presidency, attendance remains stagnant. It happens when a Micah type accepts a position in his congregation and discovers that its dynamics are very different from the business environment he comes from, and movement, if there is any, will be much slower than he wished.

The dynamic of burnout brings frustration and disillusionment, as well as a loss of energy. Indeed, if the passion is high, then the threat of burnout is also high.

STRESSORS AND THE STRESS RESPONSE

Stressors are things that happen that are external to the church leader. Sometimes chosen but often imposed, stressors impact the church leader's total person: mind, body, and spirit. A stressor may come from being in a position of chairing a meeting, delivering a speech, or teaching a class. A stressor may be a looming financial crisis or shortfall, a loss or gain of church members, an opportunity for one congregation to partner with other congregations for a social ministry outreach. A stressor may be going to the gym to work out, taking a continuing education class, or running for a regional church office and being elected or defeated. A stressor may be a violent thunderstorm, an unfavorable or favorable medical diagnosis, or getting ready for a vacation. A stressor is anything that challenges the status quo of a person's life, and it can be a positive or a negative experience.

The stress response is how the individual reacts to the stressor. Physiological changes occur in order to meet the stressor. This is often referred to as the alarm or arousal stage. A problem is seen and the threat is identified. The whole person—body, mind, and spirit—gets ready for the challenge. When the threat is met and the stress is eased, the body returns to a more normal stage where blood pressure returns to its regular resting state, pulse rate slows, and muscles relax. This rhythm—stressor, stress response, and return to a normal state—is a regular part of life.

Some stressors are chosen, such as physical exercise, taking a trip, running for office, or enrolling in a continuing education class. Some are not chosen, such as very heavy freeway traffic, congregational financial shortfalls, or a negative medical diagnosis. The more that stressors are self-chosen, the more personal mastery is learned. The more imposed stressors are met head-on, especially with the support of others, the more self-confidence grows. The rhythm of alarm/arousal to the return to a regular state of being is strengthened.

When alarm/arousal becomes a chronic state, however, the whole person—body, mind, and spirit—wears down, much like a machine does if it continuously runs at the maximum level. Parts wear out faster. It is this dynamic that church leaders could face: too many stressors form a phalanx of leadership challenges, and a constant state of stress is experienced. When the alarm/arousal stage is locked in place, the leader burns out.

Lydia had served as the administrative assistant in the parish office for ten years. During that time, the parish grew from about two hundred members to well over four hundred. A director of Christian education was added to the staff to focus on youth and family activities and, as a result, lots of new families were starting to visit the church.

"She is doing a terrific job," Lydia told the counselor her doctor referred her to, "but there is a lot more work to do now than there was when I began, and there is no additional support staff. Last week the congregation voted to call an associate pastor to focus on discipleship and the pastoral duties that are getting to be too much for the pastor, since there are so many more members.

"I keep saying there is much, much, much more to do to keep this office running well," she continued. "And people are not responding very much when I tell them that. So we get a new associate pastor because they recognize that there is too much work for one pastor, but they don't see the same thing for the office work. My doctor tells me my blood pressure and heart rate are up; I have begun to lose my temper with my kids. And I'm just not as satisfied with my work as I once was. Maybe I should look for another, less stressful job."

Lydia's blood pressure is elevated and her interpersonal resilience is lowered, evidenced by her impatience with her children and overall dissatisfaction with her job. The stressors are clear; her stress response of alarm/arousal is becoming locked in; she is on her way to leaving her job or developing a physical illness. Her response is exaggerated because she is not receiving support and understanding from others, which is necessary to help her deal with the stressors.

SECONDARY TRAUMATIC STRESS

Lydia's story continues, and as it does, the cumulative effect of stressors builds. Current stressors are magnified by their connection to past stressors. This buildup of smaller stressors, or the direct connection of a current happening to a previous traumatic one, is often called secondary traumatic stress. The buildup for Lydia could be a number of unresolved stressors throughout the ten years of her work or could be connected to previous experiences in her life.

Lydia's medical doctor recommended that she see a counselor because of her elevated blood pressure and heart rate. She still remembers that conversation with her doctor. After reviewing the results of regular testing during her annual physical and noting the blood pressure that had been climbing over the last couple of years, her doctor asked, "Anything going on in your life that would stress you and push your blood pressure higher?"

That question opened the floodgates of conversation about Lydia's job. That was a very emotional moment for Lydia, but it helped her see the real stressors of her job. The referral to a counselor was something of a shock but also something of a relief.

"One more thing," she told the counselor. "When I was growing up, I remember both my mom and my dad coming home from work exhausted. When they let their hair down to talk about their work, usually around a family gathering with my uncles and aunts, they talked about having more and more demands placed on them with less and less help available. I always thought that this was one of the things that brought on my dad's heart attack. We lost him when he was sixty-three. My mom always said that she thought it was his job that actually killed him."

"So his death—by overwork, you and your mom think—was a great loss to you both, and you wonder if what happened to him might happen to you," said Dr. Gwen, Lydia's counselor.

"I am afraid that I will repeat his history," related Lydia, "and I'll die and no longer be around for my children. You know, Dr. Gwen, this fear has been gnawing away at me for the last year or so. I get more and more frightened. It didn't help at all when I saw the church leadership turning away from my need. It was just like how my mom and dad talked about their jobs."

The stressor of the present time was linked to a very strong past trauma: her father's sudden death. In the next weeks, Lydia and her counselor began to unpack this connection. As Lydia grew stronger, she was able to more assertively confront the pastor and the congregation's leadership about her situation. Merely understanding the connection was not enough, because the actual stressor was real and needed attention. However, understanding the connection gave Lydia more resolve to confront her concern.

"We're getting ready to form a Worker Support Team," said Jill, the chair of the church personnel committee. "I promise you that the first WST that is formed will walk with you, work to understand your concerns, and advocate on your behalf for changes that all of us decide are necessary."

A Worker Support Team is discussed more fully in chapter 8 of *Holding Up the Prophet's Hand*. "The central charge of the Worker Support Team is to encourage, foster, advocate, and plan for the health and well-being of church staff in authentic partnership and conversation with them."[13]

There are many vulnerabilities, challenges, and opportunities that come along the way for church leaders. Some have common characteristics (although their specific content may differ) that are naturally part of the life of church leaders.

In order to raise up church leaders who are able to participate in building up the Body of Christ, impediments to raising up, supporting, and strengthening church leaders must be addressed specifically, forthrightly, and intentionally. To build up the Body of Christ most effectively, church leaders need to know what things have the power to tear them down and where Satan may be able exploit them. Being aware of these things as foundational challenges should help church leaders develop strategies to deal with them before and as they come up.

Supporting church leaders; encouraging healthy life patterns; attending to spiritual warfare; learning about stressors, stress responses, and secondary traumatic stress; attending to burnout—these are all things that are part of the warp and woof of community life among people who care for one another, knowing that Christ cares for them. These themes will thread throughout the book.

SPEAKING PERSONALLY

I am grateful that both Chris Asbury and Ethan Luhman graciously agreed to contribute to this book. The church needs people who are willing, like these colleagues were, to share their experiences openly and forthrightly. Church leaders all need to find more places and ways to do so and to lead the way in this sharing.

I hope I can follow their example a bit, at least, in this book. For me, this experience combines all four of these challenge areas, to some extent

---

13 Hartung, *Holding Up the Prophet's Hand*, 104.

at least. When I first came to Concordia Seminary, I attended chapel sometimes. When there were other things that I thought needed to be done, I chose to deal with them and did not participate in chapel daily.

All that changed when I became dean of ministerial formation. In that position, I drew much closer to our seminarians and sometimes to their spouses and children. I learned more of their own spiritual battles, of their challenges in coming to and being in seminary, of how different their picture of being a seminarian was from how life actually was as a seminarian. Learning more of what was naturally so on campus began to wear on me. What people experienced was not particularly unusual in a human community, nor was it much of an actual surprise. But I had drawn closer to all this, and the buildup was substantive enough that I was losing energy and enthusiasm.

I knew what was happening from a behavioral science point of view, as I was fairly informed about stressors and secondary traumatic stress. (In fact, I taught about both.) I knew I was being challenged at a burn-out level as well because there were so many things I hoped to tackle—motivators to my accepting the position in the first place. I discovered that what I was missing was the spiritual warfare component. Clearly, if all this were to continue, I would have decreasing energy to attend to the concerns of the seminarians, which would make me less effective in building up the Body of Christ.

As it became clearer to me through conversation with others that this was a place of exploitation to be used as a point of attack, it also became clear that my chapel attendance pattern needed to change. Weekly participation in the Eucharist on campus became nonnegotiable; chapel attendance became requisite. I was worshiping daily on campus with the community and was receiving the Word daily and Eucharist weekly. My life changed; I became more energized, and I believe, in that process, the demons fled, at least until they could find something else in me to exploit. Thanks be to God!

More reading? Try *Holding Up the Prophet's Hand.*

Jack felt obliged to forgive and mumbled something to that effect. But he thought, "This is exactly the issue, and we do need to talk about this."

As they settled into chairs, Pastor asked, "So, Jack, what is it you wish to discuss?"

"This is a little hard for me," Jack began, "but I want to tell you that I am having some heartburn about how you and I are working together. I want to share it with you and hope to help strengthen our work."

"Okay. Let me have it," Pastor Tom said.

"Well, for example, I raise a question with you, you promise to get back to me, and then you don't until I remind you. And like today, we agree to meet at a specific time, just like we agree to begin an elders meeting, but you don't show up on time. These may be small issues, but the repetition has been building up over time. It's hard to trust your commitment." Jack took a deep breath. He'd said it. Now what?

"Yeah," Pastor Tom responded quickly, "I am somewhat that way. My wife gets on me all the time about this when I tell her I am going to pick up the kids or reserve some time for the two of us and then I end up not doing it or being late. So don't take this personally. This is just the way I am. And in order to work well with me, people will just have to get used to it. After all, we are all sinners. I hope you will continue to forgive me."

"Well," replied a somewhat stunned Jack, "I am glad to hear that it is not personally directed at me or at the elders as a group. I suppose that is good news. I guess what I am hearing is that this is characteristic of you, and people—in this case, me—just have to get used to it."

"It's the way I've been all my life," responded Pastor Tom with a bit of an edge to his voice. "I guess you and the elders will just have to tie me down to try to make me a different person," he said with a chuckle. "Oh, I forgot to tell you this at the beginning, but I do have to cut our meeting short. I need to be at another appointment, and I don't want to be late. Please excuse me."

"Okay. I just wanted to share my thoughts with you," Jack said softly.

"Thanks for doing that," said Pastor Tom as he stretched out his hand to shake Jack's.

"Anytime."

Jack and his brother had agreed to meet for lunch after the meeting. "How did it go?" Jeff asked.

"Really lousy," said Jack. "Basically, he told me that this is the way he is, that he will not change, and that I and others should get used to it because it is part of working with him. Also, he said that I should forgive him or excuse him whenever it happens. The way it worked out, he told me he would continue not to be responsible for what he agreed to do. How can I trust him on anything?"

As Steven M. R. Covey states, "It's the little things—a day at a time, a weak or dishonest act at a time—that gradually weaken and corrode credibility."[14]

Erik Erikson, the great-grandfather of developing ways to talk about individual development in life stages, puts trust (and its opposite, mistrust) at the beginning stage of development. How do infants learn trust so they believe that the world into which they are born is relatively safe? Erikson calls this stage "trust versus mistrust," because the world is not totally safe.[15] The task of life learning at this stage is to balance the two responses and to learn both to trust and mistrust appropriately.

But how does an infant learn to trust? By having reliable parental responses to such things as hunger, discomfort, and fright. Trustworthiness, demonstrated behaviorally, teaches trust. This is not classroom learning; it is powerful learning born of experience. While infants do not have these cognitive processes available, visceral learning occurs in a preverbal way. If infants could speak, they might be say something like this: "Is the person who takes care of me ever going to get here? I am wet on my bottom and hungry in my tummy. Maybe something has happened. Maybe she doesn't like me anymore because I am crying. If she doesn't come, I would be alone in the world and have to fend for myself."

---

14 Covey, *The Speed of Trust*, 47.

15 This concept was first introduced by Erikson in his book *Identity: Youth and Crisis*.

But the parent or caregiver does arrive, hopefully sooner rather than later. Hunger is satiated, discomfort is eased, and fear is abolished. Being warmly held, fed, and changed, the infant acknowledges that life is pretty good and has great potential.

But what if the parent or caregiver arrives only after long, long minutes of crying? What if the parent or caregiver simply waits until the child is exhausted and falls asleep from fatigue? What if, when the parent or caregiver arrives, he or she is out of sorts and treats the child roughly? The infant might draw the following conclusions: "My caregiver is unreliable, maybe even dangerous, and is not likely to care well for me. I need to be careful. This may be what life is like."

Trust, initially, is learned preverbally. It emerges through the infant's emotional response to the caregiver's behavior that communicates, "I am here; life is and will be okay. I'll take care of you and provide for your needs. You can trust me because I am trustworthy." In this way, as the child matures, he becomes able to trust and finds the world more trustworthy (not perfectly!) than not.

Later, in the adored game of peekaboo, for example, the child continues to learn trust. The parent is there; the parent disappears; the parent returns. The game is predictable and fun. It is behavioral. In psychological literature, this is formally known as learning object constancy, which means that a relationship with a person is reliable even if one cannot see that person. This is a more developed level of trust. Even if the parent or caretaker is not seen or even not present, he or she will return, and, indeed, the relationship is secure and is trustworthy.

Throughout this process, home and parents become, experientially and behaviorally, safe places and reliable relationships. Trust continues to develop.

However, blind trust should not be established. Trust must be balanced by mistrust. Children, as soon as they are cognitively able, are taught about "stranger danger." Children begin to learn discernment. "Who can I trust?" becomes a life-long process of experimentation and learning. Sometimes mistakes are made on both sides of the equation: people who should not be trusted are, and people who should be trusted are not. But as this discernment process is learned in the home, in the classroom, and among peers, the capacity to accurately choose between trust and mistrust is developed as children mature.

People enter into relationships with others at different levels of the capacity to trust and to mistrust. Too much on the trusting side, and people are gullible followers of a captivating strong leader or a beguiling salesperson. Too much on the mistrusting side, and people are distant and cautious, assessing almost every behavior for signs of false steps that will cause more anxiety and higher boundaries.

Jack's positive life development and the responsiveness of trustworthy parents, teachers, church workers, and pastors made it possible, under the guidance of the Holy Spirit, for him to risk approaching Pastor Tom. If he had a higher level of mistrust, it is more likely that Jack would have simply turned away from the relationship with Pastor Tom or even become an antagonist. Both Jack's present response and the one that would have come with more mistrust would have been in response to the same style of Pastor Tom's behavior. In this case, Jack did approach Pastor Tom. Good for him!

When Jack approached Pastor Tom, it was with a limited but hopeful sense of trust. What he got in return was more reason not to trust Pastor Tom. Pastor Tom's behavior was defensive and essentially said, "If you want a relationship with me, then you have to deal with me as I am because I am not going to change, and I may not even be responsive to your needs." On a more primitive level, it would be like a hungry infant crying to be fed and having a parent come with a clean diaper but not food. "I brought what I brought," the parent says to the infant. "Take what I've got and live with it!"

How different the conversation between Jack and Pastor Tom would have been if Pastor Tom's response had been different:

"Yeah," Pastor Tom responded quickly, "I am somewhat that way. My wife gets on me all the time about this when I tell her I am going to pick up the kids or reserve some time for the two of us and then I end up not doing it or being late. So don't take this personally. Thanks so

much for sharing your response. It is important for me to get feedback like this. It will help improve our relationship. Hearing this from you convinces me that I need to take a deeper look at this."

Then Pastor Tom looked directly into Jack's eyes. "First, I apologize. I have disrespected you and every other person with whom I have been repetitively late. But this is you and me. I apologize to you. Second, I want your help. Let's both take this up with the other elders. I will ask them, as well as you, to continue to call me on this. You will be, if you agree, my prayer and accountability partners. I want and need feedback." Pastor Tom paused.

"Pastor, I would be honored to pray for you and to offer feedback. We'll work on this together. And we can talk about this with the elders at our next meeting if you wish," said Jack.

"That's a good idea. Third," continued Pastor Tom, "our health plan has a great Employee Assistance Program. I'll call them up and schedule a couple of sessions to see if I can get a deeper hold on this." The meeting ended at its appointed time with each praying for the other.

Jack and his brother had agreed to meet for lunch. "How did it go?" Jeff asked.

"Just terrifically," Jack replied. "He appreciated and even wanted my feedback. He wants the elders to be involved to help him be accountable. I can't say enough about how well it went and how open and responsive he was."

Six months later, it was clear to Jack and all the elders that Pastor Tom was working at changing. He remained open to the feedback that the elders gave him, for they needed to be trustworthy also, since they gave their word they would help. The relationship was not yet perfect, and perhaps never, in this life, would be. But there was greater respect and trust among them all.

A foundation of both teamwork and human relationships is trust, the relative absence of which is a root cause of what Peter Lencioni calls "dysfunctions" of a team. "Team members who are not genuinely open with one another about their mistakes and weaknesses make it impossible to build a foundation of trust."[16] Interpersonal trust is learned and takes time. It can never be just asserted; for example, when one person says, "Trust me." It is earned by being trustworthy. It is earned by behavior, not by assertion.

Trustworthiness includes vulnerability and honesty. Lencioni says it this way:

> Vulnerability-based trust is predicated on the single—and practical—idea that people who aren't afraid to admit the truth about themselves are not going to engage in the kind of political behavior that wastes everyone's time and energy, and more important, makes the accomplishment of results an unlikely scenario.[17]

And, of course, trust must be reinforced and learned over and over again. It is, however, always behavioral. People are worthy of trust because, by and large, they behave in trustworthy ways. People are not worthy of trust because, by and large, they behave in untrustworthy ways.

Stephen Covey takes this even further, assessing the level of a "mistrust tax" on organizations. "When trust is high, the dividend you receive is like a performance multiplier, elevating and improving every dimension of your organization and your life. High trust is like the leaven in the bread, which lifts everything around it."[18]

One of the key behaviors that Covey suggests is necessary for a person to be rightly perceived as trustworthy is to extend trust to others, often taking the initiative to trust, even when there is risk involved. Trust needs to be experienced before it can be reciprocated. He summarizes it this way:

> Demonstrate a propensity to trust. Extend trust abundantly to those who have earned your trust. Extend trust conditionally to those who are earning your trust. Learn how

---

16 Lencioni, *The Five Dysfunctions of a Team*, 188.

17 Lencioni, *The Five Dysfunctions of a Team*, 14.

18 Covey, *The Speed of Trust*, 19.

to appropriately extend trust to others based on the situation, risk, and credibility (character and competence) of the people involved. But have a propensity to trust. Don't withhold trust because there is a risk involved.[19]

In highlighting this, Covey stands in the Erik Erikson tradition of balancing trust and mistrust.

There are many personal dynamics that get in the way of having, as Covey states, "a propensity to trust." One of them is the psychological mechanism of projection, which is the defensive response to project onto others the very things that a person is dealing with himself. For instance, if a person is having difficulty dealing with angry feelings and is not able to take responsibility for those feelings, the anger can be projected onto others. In that situation, a person may not say, "I am angry," but rather, "They are angry."

In the same way, if church leaders struggle with trusting themselves and their own credibility, they may project that lack of trust onto others.

Ted was having a lot of difficulty at work. He was constantly late in finishing his assignments, even when he committed to a deadline after consulting with his supervisors. He had plausible reasons for the delays, and it seemed that he genuinely believed that the delays were repeatedly caused by outside forces. His annual evaluation made the timeliness question a major concern for necessary improvement. Ted thought he was being misunderstood.

Ted was also active in his church and was the chair of the building and grounds committee. As the chair, he held strict charge of the committee meetings and, when a project was decided upon, he micromanaged the project to make sure that it was done on time and correctly. Some of the committee members chafed at his leadership because they believed that his micromanaging projects they had responsibility for meant that he did not trust them. The consequence was that hard feelings were developing between the committee members and Ted.

---

19 Covey, *The Speed of Trust*, 229.

Ted's real difficulty, and the cause of his persistent micromanaging of projects at the church for which others had responsibility, was that underneath it all, he did not trust himself. What he experienced in himself was that he would commit to the deadline for a project, but he could not trust himself to deliver on his promise. This distrust of himself was transferred to his lack of trust of others.

The fundamental question that a church leader asks is, "Basically, do I trust myself?" To answer yes does not require that one is 100 percent trusting of oneself. In a fallen world, there are times when people cannot follow through and, therefore, let themselves or others down. Healthy church leaders recognize that and work to repair the trust damage that has occurred. The repair often takes the form of assuming responsibility and apologizing. The repair also takes the form of getting the help necessary to become more consistent in one's follow-through by developing accountability processes, among other steps.

By developing greater accountability, by letting others know that the church leader is addressing follow-through and reparations when situations have not gone well, church leaders gain an increasing level of self-trust, which translates into being able to extend trust to others. Trustworthiness begets trustworthiness; credibility begets credibility; keeping commitments begets others keeping their commitments. Unfortunately, the opposite is also true.

How wonderful it is for church leaders to know that God in Christ is trustworthy, keeps all commitments, and is completely credible. Through the power of the Holy Spirit, these characteristics become those also of the church leader. Basic to building up the Body of Christ is church leadership that is trustworthy and that extends trust to others. None of this is possible without a God who is totally and unambiguously trustworthy.

SPEAKING PERSONALLY

The scribes and Pharisees jump out here. When speaking of them, Jesus says, "So do and observe whatever they tell you, but not the works they do. For they preach, but do not practice" (Matthew 23:3). How wonderful it is that God in Christ practices the love and care that is preached by His prophets, disciples, and Jesus Himself.

Were I to be judged by emails that have gone astray or have been unanswered, correspondence that was untimely written, and promises that I failed to keep, I would certainly be judged harshly. Part of what I have learned to do, albeit imperfectly, is to agree to do only that which I know I have the capacity to do. And when I fail to do what I have agreed to do, I must and do take responsibility for it (no devil-made-me-do-it language), apologize, and work to do better.

Life is full of promises, explicit and implicit. Will I be able to keep my word? When a colleague and I agree to a deadline, will I deliver on my end of the agreement? Writing this book is a good example. It was delayed for a year, and then again for a month. It was my delay. Do you think my editor has a lot of confidence in my ability to deliver on the last deadline I established? He is cautious. He has a right to be. I can say "Trust me this time" all I want, but I really do need to deliver.

I believe that I am not the only church leader who struggles with this. If you do, read further. I suggest Stephen Covey's book *The Speed of Trust: The One Thing That Changes Everything* as a next step. I found it to be extremely helpful because it takes up this core topic:

> When you trust people, you have confidence in them—in their integrity and in their abilities. When you distrust people, you are suspicious of them—of their integrity, their agenda, their capabilities or their track record. It's that simple. We have all had experiences that validate the difference between relationships that are built on trust and those that are not. These experiences clearly tell us the difference is not small; it is dramatic.[20]

Indeed! Trust works both ways.

My prayer is that the Spirit continues to lead me to more trustworthy behaviors and to establish ever more increasingly trusting relationships.

---

20 Covey, *The Speed of Trust*, 5.

There the trust question is whether other people can trust that I am genuinely interested in them, in connecting well with them, and in learning about them. That leads us to the question of how I respond to them. On to the next chapter.

CHAPTER FIVE

Ways to Respond to Others

George was silent through the whole Bible class. The topic that the class was discussing was stewardship. The focus of this week's class was the use of the gift of money. Throughout the class, George grew more and more irritated. Tithing, support of others by contributions to social service agencies, honest filing of income tax returns so that governmental services can be supported—these were hot buttons for George. The pastor asserted that the money people have is really not their possession, but rather it is to be used for the general good of people and support of the work of the kingdom of God. "The pastor and religion," George thought, "have no real say in how I use my possessions. After all, I work hard for what I have."

His irritation overflowed, so after the class ended he approached the pastor and said, "I really have had enough of this talk about money. The church should stay out of everyone's private life."

What response might the pastor make in such an emotionally charged situation?

Hit with this in-your-face and angry response, Pastor David could feel his blood pressure rise and heart race. Here, he was with this angry man at the very moment that he needed to get ready for the next worship service. This whole thing was really irritating to him as well, but there was little he could do at that moment; he knew he was not thinking very clearly and his emotions were getting in the way.

Strong emotions can drive wedges between people, though not so much because they themselves exist, for emotions clearly exist. Rather, it is what we do with our emotions and how we respond to others that are the critical concerns.

These behavioral interactions between people are commonplace and are necessary, although positive behaviors have more value in connecting people. But the kind of interaction between George and Pastor David could also lead to a more vibrant and closer connection as well. In many ways, much of the quality of relationship depends on the response of Pastor David.

George has done his part to honestly and openly voice his concerns, one human being to another. He has not kept his disagreement with Pastor David to himself; he has not let it fester so that it serves as a toxic and enduring negative response; he has not shared it with anyone other than Pastor David. Granted, the delivery was not as constructive as it could have been! But he did share his inner world, his inner responses.

If George, angry or calm, had not shared his responses with Pastor David, he would not have reached out to connect honestly and transparently with him. As flawed as his outburst was, it was, nevertheless, a way to connect. And in so doing, George was making a statement concerning the relationship that he wanted to have with his pastor: honest and transparent. At the same time that his anger was boiling over, he was also connecting personally with Pastor David. The relationship was, at some level, important to him. Researcher John Gottman calls this a "bid," "the way people, in mundane moments in everyday life, make attempts at emotional communication, and how others around them respond, or fail to respond, to these attempts."[21]

Church leaders whose task is to build up the Body of Christ will recognize that most everything that involves human interaction has an

---

21 Gottman and DeClaire, *The Relationship Cure*, xi.

implication as to whether a relationship grows or withers.

Since George has done his part to honestly albeit imperfectly engage his relationship with Pastor David, it is now Pastor David's turn to respond. Following are various options.

1. IGNORE

"I don't have time to talk with you about this. I have to lead the next service." And with that, Pastor David quickly walked away, his own agitation obvious.

Here, Pastor David walks away from George's attempt to connect with him. Using the time factor—a real concern of his—Pastor David misses the personal connection and engaging qualities of George's communication and shuts it down. George's communication was met by Pastor David's barrier. Time becomes the rationale to cut off contact.

The relationship implications of Pastor David's response are significant. The message "I do not have time for you" has the potential to communicate that the importance of George's comment, the importance of George to Pastor David personally, and the importance of the relationship were quite low. Pastor David's response offers nothing in return for George's reaching out; rather, it blocks the connection.

All church leaders will do this from time to time. A single response that blocks a connecting response of another is unlikely, by itself, to break a relationship, but if the blocking response occurs in the future, it will contribute to a deepening wedge and, eventually, to a break in the relationship.

"Pastor walked away from me and didn't give me the time of day," thought an increasingly perturbed George. The thought fleetingly occurred to him, "Maybe he really doesn't care much about me." That thought made him even angrier and a little sad. He wondered if others had similar experiences with Pastor David. He spied Rasheed, a friend and also a member of the Bible class, and walked over to him to ask him if Pastor David had ever walked away like this from him. Rasheed really did not have any experiences with Pastor David like George's, but

he had seen the exchange and wondered himself about what Pastor David's response actually meant. It seemed somewhat off-putting to him.

In such ways, conversations about people pick up steam and opinions begin to form. In this case, George continues to be angry because he was, in his experience, ignored. Rasheed is now in the picture, as well. Who knows what next becomes part of a conversation generated by the brief interaction between Pastor David and George? The relationship between Pastor David and George becomes less transparent and less honest as more inner responses are kept hidden. Behavior changes as the open sharing of feelings and of thoughts is diminished. Ignoring begets more ignoring.

John Gottman calls this kind of a response "turning away" and defines it as follows: "This pattern of relating generally involves ignoring another's bid, or acting preoccupied."[22]

2. ATTACK

"Really, George, you are just captured by your self-interest, and that is not in the spirit of Jesus."

Here, Pastor David responds to the angry and confrontational part of George's attempt at connection with his own angry, attacking, and defensive response. He moves away from both an engagement of the content of the communication and an engagement of George's feelings. Instead of receiving the attempt at connection, he defends himself with an assault. Not only does he not engage the content of George's response, but he also attacks the nature of George's very being: "You are just being captured by your self-interest." Then, to add to the attack, he suggests that George is not acting in a Christian manner.

The relationship implications of this kind of a response are clear: do not approach Pastor David if you disagree with him. Keep any disagreements locked up inside. If you disagree with him, you will be subject to personal attack. In response to George's reaching out, Pastor David cast

---

22 Gottman and DeClaire, *The Relationship Cure*, 17.

a stone. Since George likely does not wish to be hurt or attacked, Pastor David's response will significantly reduce attempts at personal engagement and may confine interaction only to topics that George believes are congruent with Pastor David's opinion. Transparency and honest communication will decrease.

From time to time, all church leaders will respond this way. Left alone and not tended to, the recollection of this kind of exchange will continue to stoke George's anger. It will also contribute to the development of a defensive style of interaction. Unless the relationship and this specific instance are tended to, George will dance around Pastor David, fearful of another angry and attacking response from him.

"I guess I told him where to go," Pastor David thought as he walked away. "What right does he have to say that about what I was teaching?" Still stirred up as he entered the vestry to robe for the next service, he shared the interaction he had with George with Louis, the assisting elder. This, of course, influenced Louis, who wondered whether Pastor David was under too much stress and if George, a longtime member, was deeply dissatisfied with Pastor David's leadership. He thought he might raise his own concerns about Pastor at the next elders meeting.

"Wow, does he have a temper!" George said to Natalie, his wife, as they had lunch after church. "I think we should stay away from him and handle him with kid gloves. He must have other things going on in his life to cause him to be so edgy."

Natalie was upset and planned say something about this to Lisa, her close friend and head of the congregation's women's ministry.

This is how negative conversations about people pick up steam and opinions form. In this case, when the relationship is distanced like this, both parties may be more anxiety-prone because of the threat of an angry response and, while the relationship may continue, it will most likely never be a close one. Attack responses teach people to withhold their concerns and disagreements, as well as their hurt feelings and inner conflicts, for fear of further attack. They also encourage people to respond in attacking ways in return, as attack begets attack.

John Gottman calls this "turning against" and defines it in this way: "People who turn against one another's bids for connection might be described as belligerent or argumentative."[23]

3. CONNECT

"George, thank you for sharing your response to our work together this morning. You have a lot of feelings about this. I need to be off to prepare for the next church service now, but I would like to talk further with you about this. How about two o'clock tomorrow afternoon?"

Here, Pastor David does several things: (1) he speaks appreciatively concerning George's sharing, (2) he acknowledges George's feelings connected with the content, and (3) he acts to schedule a time when they can thoroughly discuss George's concerns face-to-face.

The relationship implications of this type of behavior are also clear: (1) respect for the position of the other person, (2) respect for and awareness of the feelings connected with the conversation, and (3) acknowledgment of the importance of the relationship and of the person, evidenced by a desire to talk more deeply about the concerns that trouble George.

All church leaders will, from time to time, do this. As church leaders grow in their personal and leadership skills, they will respond this way more often. This kind of response sets the groundwork for Pastor David to develop a closer relationship with George. It sets a tone that will increase the number of transparent and authentic communications between them.

"George sure had some strong feelings about our class this morning. I wonder what that was all about. I am glad we could schedule time tomorrow to talk about it. I am thankful that he is willing to speak his mind with me, and I pray that the Spirit will guide our conversation. Besides, the additional time will help me calm down too," thought Pastor David.

---

23 Gottman and DeClaire, *The Relationship Cure*, 17.

"Do you know what Pastor David did when I talked to him after class today?" George said to Natalie as they were having lunch after church. "I was pretty riled up about our class, and got on his case pretty good, but he recognized that I had an issue with it all and we scheduled a time tomorrow to talk about it. I think this is pretty great. I don't know how the conversation will go, but I do know that he respected me and responded to me. So, I expect that the time will go well. Besides, the additional time will help me calm down."

Natalie was pleased because she knew of George's tendency to get, as he said, "riled up," and she knew that it was good that he was going to talk further with Pastor David. She would share how pleased she was that this was happening with Lisa, her close friend and head of the congregation's women's ministry.

In such ways, conversations about people pick up steam and opinions form. In this case, the relationship between George and Pastor David has the potential to become closer, more transparent, and more authentic. The conversation has the capacity to build up the individuals and to build up the relationship between them as well. As thoughts and feelings are expressed and responded to (not necessarily agreed with), people are encouraged to share more often. Empathic connection begets more connection. Clearly, interactions do not always go well, even in this kind of a context. But when there is empathic connection, there is always opportunity for repair.

John Gottman calls this "turning toward" and defines it simply: "to react in a positive way to another's bids for emotional connection."[24]

When the people of the Body of Christ are not nourished in positive, connecting ways, their relationships and vitality languish. Church leaders need both to be nourished themselves and to nourish others.

This ongoing process of reaching out also applies in our relationship with God. A basic human need is to be nourished by God in Christ. At times we, perhaps like the psalmist, struggle for such nourishment. The verses "Give ear to my prayer, O God, and hide not Yourself from

---

24 Gottman, *The Relationship Cure*, 16.

my plea for mercy!" (Psalm 55:1) and "O God, hear my prayer; give ear to the words of my mouth" (Psalm 54:2) both give expression to the psalmist's need (and he does speak for all us) to be connected with God in such a way that God's response is neither anger nor disregard.

The distance from God, the psalmist's cry for connection, and the results of the distance between the psalmist and God are clearly identified:

> Hear my prayer, O LORD; let my cry come to You! Do not hide Your face from me in the day of my distress! Incline Your ear to me; answer me speedily in the day when I call! For my days pass away like smoke, and my bones burn like a furnace. My heart is struck down like grass and has withered; I forget to eat my bread. Because of my loud groaning my bones cling to my flesh. . . . For I eat ashes like bread and mingle tears with my drink, because of Your indignation and anger; for You have taken me up and thrown me down. My days are like an evening shadow; I wither away like grass." (Psalm 102:1–5, 9–11)

This sounds like depression, weight loss, loss of appetite, and, perhaps, arthritis.

This is what happens without connection with God; this is also what happens without positive human connections. Effective responses that build up rather than tear down are vital, and behavioral leadership by church leaders is so vital as well.

What if all of our congregations' members were taught such responsive skills and behaved in ways that actively and creatively used them? Congregations would certainly then be places where people connect in ways that are mutually responsive, encouraging, supportive, and helpful. They would be places of coming together, where people know one another more deeply and support and help each other more actively. They would be places where life experiences are shared and positive emotions are engaged. They would be places where creativity is encouraged and outreach is cultivated. They would be places where values of authenticity, openness, transparency, empathy, and unity are fostered and encouraged. They would be places where people live at the foot of the cross, in the power of Christ's empty tomb, and with the enlightenment and energy of the Holy Spirit.

But how is this taught?

One way is by the witness and example of church leaders whose behavior is responsive to others. This is not something that is taught in an academic sense and, therefore, is not really taught in this book. It is taught by the lived lives of members of the Body of Christ, especially those who lead.

Brice noticed that Sam was slumped over as he was sitting in the worship service. He looked tired and maybe—Brice did not know for sure—sad. This was not the Sam that Brice knew. Sam was a guy who stood tall and straight and, while not exceptionally outgoing, had a sense of brightness and energy about him.

As soon as the service was over, Brice went over to Sam, put his hand on his shoulder, and said, "Something up?"

Sam looked up and their eyes met. "Yeah."

"I've got a few minutes now to talk. If you have a couple of minutes, and you are willing, let's find a place to chat," said Brice. They found a spot in the corner of one of the classrooms. "What's going on?" Brice asked.

"Well . . . ," said Sam, and the conversation was off and running.

***

Leo was reading the paper in the few spare moments he had between arriving home after work and before dinner. The article was pretty interesting. Just then, Alice, his sixth-grade daughter, popped through the door and exclaimed, "Dad! I got my report card today."

Leo immediately put the newspaper down. "Let me see," he responded. The sharing, conversation, and happiness were off and running.

In small and large ways, people respond in empathic connection to one another and, in doing so, they nourish one another. In this way, followers of Christ, blessed by the Spirit of God, build one another up.

Speaking Personally

John Gottman's book *The Relationship Cure* is one of the most helpful introductory books on personal relationships that I have found. Thus, I recommend it as the next-step reading to pursue the ideas contained in this chapter. One of the premier marriage and family researchers in the United States, Gottman's *The Seven Principles for Making Marriage Work* is also a classic. In both cases, the reader will need to discern appropriately (as is always the case); there will be things readers may not agree with in each of these books. But the overall value of *The Relationship Cure* and *The Seven Principles for Making Marriage Work* cannot be overstated.

The focus on empathic responsiveness has helped me in the context of reframing the nature of human connections. For instance, I never much thought that an angry approach could be helpful. But even anger speaks to relationship. Once I learned that, it was much easier for me to hear people out.

I also learned that I will always mess this up. There is no way that I am perfectly responsive all the time. I often need to repair what I have missed. Following up when I become aware that I have ignored or attacked another person, I am now in a position to work toward repair. "I am really sorry that I did not pay much attention to you" or "I let my anger override my care for you, and I am sorry I did that" opens the door for repair. Frankly, this is not so easy for me to do. I was raised in a family where, generally, we just went on and ignored what had happened. To go back and seek repair is difficult. But I have found that it is necessary for my relationships with others to continue to thrive. I am so thankful that God in Christ neither ignored nor attacked, but connected intimately and personally with humankind to repair and redeem the world.

Once empathic connection is made and repairs (if needed) are also made, what is next? We'll see in the next chapter.

Listening, the First Service We Owe

Empathic connection to others naturally leads to opportunities to understand them more deeply and intimately, to walk with them more
closely, and to be more helpful, useful, and supportive. Basic listening
skills and attitudes are necessary to better understand another person.
Fundamental to leadership of most any kind, and certainly church leadership in particular, is the capacity of the leader to pay attention and
listen. It is through listening that we understand a fuller picture of what
is being communicated. Michael Nichols puts it this way:

> Few motives in human experience are as powerful as the
> yearning to be understood. Being listened to means that
> we are taken seriously, that our ideas and feelings are rec-
> ognized, and, ultimately that what we have to say matters.
> The yearning to be heard is a yearning to escape our
> isolation and bridge the space that separates us.[25]

Dietrich Bonhoeffer offers the following observation in his book *Life
Together*:

> The first service that one owes to others in the fellowship
> consists in listening to them. Just as love to God begins

---

25 Nichols, *The Lost Art of Listening*, 9.

with listening to His Word, so the beginning of love for the brethren is learning to listen to them. It is God's love for us that He not only gives us His Word but also lends us His ear. So it is His work that we do for our brother when we learn to listen to him.[26]

There are many communication skills (illustrated below), all of which are useful for church leaders and need to be used at different times.

"Whose need to talk is greater?"

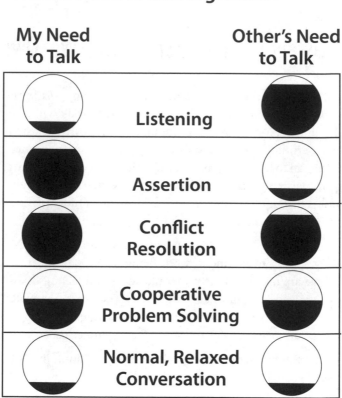

Ridge Consultants, Cazenovia, New York

---

26 Bonhoeffer, *Life Together*, 97.

Listening makes all the other skills work. Therefore, listening skills are essential for church leaders who wish to engage the thoughts, ideas, and emotions of the person to whom they are speaking. Church leaders can do things that get in the way of this most basic aspect of the development and building of strong relationships. "Listening is so basic that we take it for granted. Unfortunately, most of us think of ourselves as better listeners than we really are."[27]

It is easy for one person to assert that he or she understands another. But that is not necessarily the case. Listening, like trustworthiness, must always be demonstrated.

Deaconess Sara went to visit Cynthia, a hospitalized elderly church member. She did not know Cynthia well, since Sara had taken her position in her parish only three months before.

Cynthia was hospitalized with, according to some, the final stages of her cancer. After a few minutes of introductory discussion, Deaconess Sara, turning the conversation toward Cynthia, asked how Cynthia was doing.

She replied, "I know the end is near. I know God will take me and I will be with Jesus. But I am worried that my husband, John, will not be able to go on. He relies on me for so much. Can you understand that, Deaconess?"

"I understand how you feel," said Deaconess Sara, "and I am sure that God will take care of John."

*"But does she really, **really** understand?" thought Cynthia.*

"I want to share with you a Bible verse that speaks to this," continued Deaconess Sara.

Time will tell how this conversation will turn out. Cynthia's thought—her question—was an important one. It is one thing for Deaconess Sara to say that she understands. Frankly, anyone can make such an assertion about almost anything. The important question is whether the person truly does understand and can demonstrate that this is so. What is necessary is the demonstration of the understanding that has occurred,

---

27 Nichols, *The Lost Art of Listening*, 12.

not the assertion of it. This is why listening is a skill that needs to be demonstrated.

"I know the end is near. I know God will take me and I will be with Jesus. But I am worried that my husband, John, will not be able to go on. He relies on me for so much. Can you understand that, Deaconess?"

"Let's see if I can get close to what you were saying. You are confident that you are now and will be forever with Jesus. Also, though, you are anxious—you said worried—that John will not be able to move on well without you," said Deaconess Sara in a soothing tone.

"Yes," said Cynthia, practically interrupting Deaconess Sara. "I remember a time that I went off by myself to visit my sister, and when I got home the house was in a mess and John said he hadn't had a good meal in three days."

Time will tell how this conversation will turn out as well. But what Deaconess Sara did was demonstrate that she was paying attention, tracking the conversation and listening well. Reflecting both the feelings and the content of Cynthia's statement gave evidence that Deaconess Sara was listening and understanding. The effectiveness of Sara's response prompted Cynthia to offer more information. In this case, it was a recollection of a time when she left John on his own, albeit only for a brief time. Now she contemplates leaving for a forever-until-we-meet-again-in-heaven time. Her worry about John is as important, if not more important, than her concern about her own death.

Listening is important as a first service because it gives people the opportunity to share what is important to them and gives church leaders an opportunity to demonstrate that they are truly and experientially alongside them. Listening skills used by church leaders demonstrate that the leader understands both the thoughts and feelings of the person who is speaking, and that the leader understands these in the context of the world as the speaker sees it, and not only as the leader sees it.

Listening is essential to make any other communication skill work. But there are many things that get in the way. Here are some common stumbling blocks, with examples in the context of the conversation between Deaconess Sara and Cynthia:

1. Early general questions, such as "Please tell me how you are doing," or "I would like to know how it is going with you," are invitations to talk about substantive matters. As such, they are often necessary to set the tone of the conversation. But a lot of information-gathering questions, one right after another, put the questioner in a position of control and place the impetus of the conversation squarely on the questioner. The church leader takes charge of the conversation; the other person is simply the responder and takes on a more passive role. *"How old is John?"* and *"Is John depressed?"* and *"Have the doctors told you that the end is near?"* are all examples of such questions. Cynthia would likely answer them, but Deaconess Sara has taken over the conversation and its direction. Information may be gathered, but questions like these are the areas of interest to the questioner, not necessarily what Cynthia wants or needs to discuss.

2. Turning the conversation away from the person's context to the church leader's context. Telling a parallel story is another form of seizing control of the conversation. *"My dad had the same kind of feelings when he was near his end, but my mom was able to work through his death pretty well, sad as she was to lose him."* While this kind of response might seem like an empathic one, especially in the early stages of the conversation it turns the attention from Cynthia to Deaconess Sara. If the conversation continues this kind of sharing pattern, Cynthia will not move as deeply into her needs. Church leaders should place full attention on the experience and context of the person and seek to understand the person's experience by focusing on how the other person is feeling.

3. Advice too early. Often neither the presenting issue nor the first statements concerning what is happening are really driving the concern. Attention to underlying or seemingly background concerns is critical to understanding the situation. Focusing on the first concern and attempting to give advice about it often stops further exploration into areas that may be more central. Advice may

help the church leader feel useful, but if it misses the essential and core concern, it obviously will not be as helpful. *"Just pray that John will be given the strength to continue on,"* or *"I want to share with you a Bible verse that speaks to this,"* are examples of this. Additionally, sometimes people just want to be heard and understood, and advice is not what they seek.

4. Inattention to the environment. In order for active listening to occur, there need to be conversation boundaries and minimal distractions. An attentive discussion in the midst of a lot of other people, for instance, may not be possible and may need to move to a more private space. In the case of the conversation between Cynthia and Deaconess Sara, potential barriers to an attentive discussion might be other family members who want to speak for Cynthia or medical personnel who may come in. Asking for some one-on-one time together apart from staff and family might help solve this.

5. Inattention to personal emotional availability and openness. The church leader might not be in an emotional position to be in listening mode. For instance, if Deaconess Sara has recently experienced the death of someone close to her, she may still be grieving and find it difficult to offer Cynthia the listening ear she needs. Or if Deaconess Sara has just had a confrontation with someone else, she might be distracted, agitated, and less able to listen. Deaconess Sara must always be aware of her own whole-person health before she can offer care to another. She may consider debriefing with a trusted colleague before making the hospital call, for example.

6. Holding onto an agenda. The church leader may have an agenda with someone. It could be to have the other person support a particular position, agree with a particular value, or take sides in a conflict. In this case, conversation is influenced by the church leader's agenda in a way that interferes with his or her objective listening. The discussion takes place within the context of the agenda rather than in the service of more deeply understanding the person.

Robert Bolton suggests that there are six "peculiarities" of human communication:

1. Words have different meanings for different people.

2. People often "code" their messages.

3. People frequently talk about the "presenting problem," when another topic is of greater concern to them.

4. The speaker may be blind to his or her emotions or be blinded by them.

5. Listeners are often easily distracted.

6. Listeners hear through "filters" that distort much of what is being said.[28]

These common peculiarities necessitate an active-listening approach to form the foundation of good human relationships and good church leadership. Church leaders will want to be sure that words spoken in the conversation have the same meaning to each person; they will want to decode the conversation so that what is being talked about is clear; they will want to explore the initial presentation of a concern or an idea to see if there are underlying concerns; they will seek to connect feelings to thoughts and thoughts to feelings so that parties to a conversation can connect better; they will seek to focus on what is being discussed; they will search for the implicit meanings that people put on what they see and clarify those meanings.

The act of listening is to give full attention to the message the other person is communicating. A response of one person to another that includes both thoughts that were heard and feelings that were expressed is truly a reflective response that is holistic in nature.

As people learn to use listening skills, they may feel that their reflecting responses are somewhat wooden and repetitive. This is most often because they are reflecting on the content only or that their reflections come too quickly or too often and actually disrupt the conversation. Effective reflecting in a conversation will briefly state the core of what the person has communicated, incorporating both content and feeling. The

---

28 Bolton, *People Skills*, 78.

image of a mirror is a good one for this process. Not only are the church leaders stepping into the world and the picture of it that other people have, but the church leaders are also seeking to understand that world in both feeling (emotional) and thinking (ideational) dimensions.

When there is too much emphasis on what people are thinking, feelings can be undervalued or even disregarded. However, feelings also need recognition because they are important in the life of a person and are essential to seeing a larger picture of what is happening. Tying the feelings to the thoughts by responding with comments like "You feel disappointed and irritated because the promotion went to someone else" or "You seem pretty angry as you talk about the struggles you are having with your wife" are examples of effective reflecting.

The capacity to listen to others with the goal of understanding them more fully and deeply is a core skill for church leaders, as well as a basic skill for all interpersonal interaction. Such listening skills are not the only skills needed for leadership, of course, but they are the foundation for the effective use of all other skills. The goal is always to work toward strengthening empathic relationships—relationships of deeper understanding—so the rest of life's tasks may be approached more effectively.

Building on learning to be responsive and to empathically connect, church leaders seek to develop a style and mind-set where understanding is always prized and deeper understanding is always sought. Greater understanding is foundationally dependent on the capacity to listen and then to demonstrate that listening by reflecting. The interaction of listening and reflecting builds relationships, and if both parties are using this, then the building becomes mutual and even stronger.

Active listening that includes reflective responses tests whether the listener is following the content, meaning, and emotion of what is being said. There are many ways to do this. One way was demonstrated by Deaconess Sara when she stated, "Let's see if I can get close to what you were saying." Here is another example of how she could have handled the same conversation:

Cynthia replied, "I know the end is near. I know God will take me and I will be with Jesus. But I am worried that my husband, John, will not be able to go on. He relies on me for so much. Can you understand that, Deaconess?"

"Here is what I am hearing you say," Deaconess Sara said. "Please tell me if I am on target . . ."

Here is another option of how it could have gone:

Cynthia replied, "I know the end is near. I know God will take me and I will be with Jesus. But I am worried that my husband, John, will not be able to go on. He relies on me for so much. Can you understand that, Deaconess?"

"I think I do," said Deaconess Sara, "but let's check that out . . ."

In these examples, Deaconess Sara did not assert that she understood, nor did she assume it. She tested her sense of understanding by communicating clearly and directly that she was going to reflect what she heard and that she wanted to know if her reflection was accurate.

When a reflection is accurate, there is often a verbal response, such as "yes" or "uh-huh," or the speaker continues offering deeper information or feelings or both, as was the case in the example conversation. When this occurs, there is wonderful opportunity for conversations to go much deeper, perhaps into arenas that are surprising. Gottman compares "such exchanges to an improvised jazz duet. Neither musician knows exactly where the piece is going, but they get their cues by tuning in to one another."[29]

Reflection is a process where the listener is in search of the deeper levels of meaning in the communication of the speaker and is always testing that understanding by speaking, in brief and summarizing ways, what he or she is hearing. Besides being brief, reflective responses should be kept within the context of the speaker's view of the world, empathetically spoken, somewhat summative, and presented as statements (not questions). Reflective responses should always present both a connection between the content of the conversation and the feelings expressed in it.

---

29 Gottman and DeClaire, *The Relationship Cure*, 40.

People generally wish to be understood, so they will usually correct listeners' misunderstandings. Listeners will be alert to these corrections and respond to them. Speakers are the experts on their lives, so they are the teachers and listeners are the learners. The task of church leaders, therefore, is to be continuous learners as others teach about themselves, their view of the world, attitudes, opinions, and emotions.

If church leaders take on the task of learning from those who are speaking, they will be alert when corrections are made. Here is one example of a correction from the conversation between Deaconess Sara and Cynthia.

"Can you understand that, Deaconess?"

"I understand how you feel," said Deaconess Sara, "and I am sure that God will take care of John."

*"Does she really, **really** understand?" thought Cynthia.*

"I want to share with you a Bible verse that speaks to this," continued Deaconess Sara.

Here, Cynthia's concern about being understood went underground. The correction was made, but it was nonverbal—Cynthia gave control of the conversation to Deaconess Sara. Sometimes, people withdraw from active participation in the conversation. If Deaconess Sara had noticed this, she may have said something like "Cynthia, you asked me if I understood and I said I did, but maybe I have missed something in what you were saying. I want to understand. Would you be willing to tell me again about your concerns about John?"

Here is a second example:

"He relies on me for so much. Can you understand that, Deaconess?"

"I understand how you feel," said Deaconess Sara, "and I am sure that God will take care of John."

Cynthia eyes darkened a bit. "I guess you're right," she said softly and then sighed.

Here, Cynthia's correction was more direct but needs to be interpreted. Deaconess Sara might have responded, "I do believe that God will care for John, but in sharing that with you, I may have missed what you were saying. You were talking about your 'worry' for him. Perhaps you could tell me more about that." Here, Deaconess Sara recognizes that something in the conversation has gone astray and seeks to get back on track.

Other kinds of corrective responses in other conversations could include "Well, sort of . . . ," "Hmm, kind of . . . ," silence that is uncomfortable, or even "Not really." The response to these statements can be framed like this:

"I missed something in what you were saying. Let's give it another try."

"Better listening doesn't start with a set of techniques. It starts with making a sincere effort to pay attention to what's going on in the other person's private world of experience."[30] So it is for church leaders. Bonhoeffer is right: the first duty we owe one another is to listen. Listening builds relationships.

SPEAKING PERSONALLY

Like all of us, I inherit the results of the tower of Babel incident. While I may speak in the same language as others around me, at times what I think they are saying is not what they are saying at all. Because of our peculiarities, we are speaking different languages. When I am in darker moments, I blame others for not speaking more clearly. When I am more in the light, so to speak, I know it is my responsibility to listen better. In the fall of humankind, even language is corrupted. But in the Body of Christ, we work confident that Christ has redeemed the world and, therefore, has redeemed our language. Spirit-motivated, I seek, imperfectly, to understand better.

Frankly, I am not a natural listener. I think, rather, that I am a natural talker. Listening is a crucial skill. I am still learning it.

Proverbs 18:2 was pointed out to me by an early reader of this chapter: "A fool takes no pleasure in understanding, but only in expressing his opinion." Daily, I need to repent of this, lest I remain a fool.

---

30 Nichols, *The Lost Art of Listening*, 140.

Good reading is Robert Bolton's *People Skills: How to Assert Yourself, Listen to Others, and Resolve Conflicts.* Robert's son, Jim, continues this fine work at www.ridge.com. Also good reading is Michael Nichols's *The Lost Art of Listening: How Learning to Listen Can Improve Relationships.* Either of these books is a great next step to investigate how to become a better listener. Stephen Ministries does a wonderful job of teaching listening skills in their training program. Look them up at www.stephenministries.org. Finally, local community colleges often have courses that teach listening skills. Go for it!

CHAPTER SEVEN

Safe Spaces

Church leaders living lives—imperfect as they may be—of trustworthiness marked by listening, centered in the forgiveness of Christ, and empowered by the Holy Spirit are in a position to extend trust to others. While mutual trust is developed as people interact with one another, the natural tendency of church leaders is both to trust others and to facilitate relationships and groups that develop mutual trust and safety.

Trust is not gained by assertion. It is gained by behavior. This is true for individual church leaders as they demonstrate trustworthiness. It is also true of groups as people grow together in relative safety. "Trust is all about vulnerability. Team members who learn how to trust each other learn to be comfortable being open, even exposed, to one another around their failures, weaknesses, even fears."[31]

This is much like St. Paul's exhortation following his section on the Body of Christ:

> Let love be genuine. Abhor what is evil; hold fast to what is good. Love one another with brotherly affection. Outdo one another in showing honor. Do not be slothful in zeal,

---

31 Lencioni, *The Five Dysfunctions of a Team*, 14.

be fervent in spirit, serve the Lord. Rejoice in hope, be patient in tribulation, be constant in prayer. Contribute to the needs of the saints and seek to show hospitality.

Bless those who persecute you; bless and do not curse them. Rejoice with those who rejoice, weep with those who weep. Live in harmony with one another. Do not be haughty, but associate with the lowly. Never be wise in your own sight. Repay no one evil for evil, but give thought to do what is honorable in the sight of all. . . . Do not be overcome by evil, but overcome evil with good. (Romans 12:9–17, 21)

It is the responsibility of church leaders to foster relationships of mutual vulnerability and trust, of careful listening and responding, all the while prayerfully asking for the blessing of the Holy Spirit in so doing. What is necessary for these relationships between members of the Body of Christ to grow?

It is certainly necessary that all members of the congregation regularly gather together around God's Word and the celebration of the sacramental Meal, where they regularly confess together, hear the word of forgiveness proclaimed to them, and are built up for works of service.

Members of the community also need places of safety where they can speak more intimately with one another about their lives, struggles, and spiritual walk. This requires vulnerability and openness. It is not possible to rejoice with those who rejoice if there is not opportunity to learn of their rejoicing; it is not possible to weep with those who weep if there is not opportunity to learn of their weeping.

David Hilton suggests that the development of authentic relationships is a major task for the churches and, therefore, of church leadership:

For me, the model of a place that welcomes people as they are is Alcoholics Anonymous. Everybody who goes says, "I've blown it," and everyone else smiles and says, "Yeah, we know what that's like. Come on in and join us." Nobody tells anybody what to do; they just share what their struggles are and what they've found that helps and doesn't help. Everybody's open about their brokenness and failure, and they heal. That process is the only thing I know of that heals addictions. What happens in most of our churches is just the opposite. We all get dressed up on Sunday, and we go there and we say, "Isn't it great, all these good people!" So I don't dare share my pain and my brokenness with you because you might reject me. We sit there with our pain and our brokenness, and we never share it and we don't heal. Our church's real challenge in the next decade or two is to find out how we can change from being congregations of pretense to being healing communities; we have to work toward becoming the kind of communities where it's safe to tell your life story.[32]

Churches today are not always environments of trust and safety. Communities of believers often struggle to become places of safety. I have noted that in another place:

If Christ's community is his gift to us; if others in his community come into our life space as his gifts; if our learning and growing as disciples is in some way dependent on our engaging with others . . . if our first task is to listen rather than to speak, to understand rather than to teach . . . if empathy—"suffer when others suffer and rejoice when others rejoice"—is central; if we are actually interrelated and engaged systemically with others whether or not we admit it or are aware of it, then what keeps us from engaging in these creative and healthy ways with others?[33]

And I believe:

Openness and honesty are foundational for authentic encounter. Authenticity, in turn, makes it possible for people to receive the words and deeds of affirmation others

---

32 David Hilton, *Second Opinion*, vol. 18, no. 3 (January 1993): n.p.

33 Bruce Hartung, "Empathy and Community," *Inviting Community* (St. Louis: Concordia Seminary Press, 2015), 59.

offer us, interpreting them as meaningful. In one-on-one conversations, in small group interactions, in boards and meetings, in Bible study and prayer, members of the Christian community have opportunities to come to know one another more deeply, authentically, and genuinely.[34]

Nevertheless, we recognize that even in the church, there are challenges to developing a place where people feel safe and trust others. Church leaders are called to facilitate an environment where congregational members are able to reveal their thoughts and feelings about their personal lives and also be open about their opinions, suggestions, and hopes for the congregation and the committees on which they may serve.

The first challenge to church leaders is that the leaders be trustworthy, as discussed in chapter 4. Without trustworthy leadership—leadership that behaves in trustworthy ways—not a lot gets accomplished. With trustworthy leadership, a foundation is laid that offers places for creative thinking and thoughtful discussion.

Gloria had served several times as president of her congregation's women's organization. A recognized and competent leader and thoughtful student of the Scriptures, she regularly attended Pastor Nathan's Sunday morning Bible class. Gloria liked Pastor Nathan, a recent seminary graduate, and found him to be friendly and intelligent. She struggled, though, because there was increasingly less discussion in the Bible class and much more lecturing. Studying the Bible had become listening to Pastor Nathan expound on the Bible. She missed the time spent in discussion that Pastor Casey, who had left the congregation a year earlier, fostered. But more than that, in the months since Pastor Nathan's Sunday school class had begun, there had been several times that members of the class questioned or challenged Pastor Nathan's understanding of a particular Bible passage.

"He just cut them off," she thought on her way to the car after class, "and suggested that they were misinformed, not knowledgeable

---

34 Hartung, *Holding Up the Prophet's Hand*, 79.

about the Scriptures, and had not been studying the Scriptures enough. He reminded us that he spent three years at the seminary and one year on vicarage and, because of this, he was the expert in the room."

She found this fairly off-putting and shared her musings with her husband, Don. "After a couple of times," she said, "people just stopped questioning, discussion fell way down, and, coincidentally, attendance has begun to drop off as well."

"Why don't you talk to Pastor Nathan about this?" Don asked.

"I don't want to be embarrassed and get verbally attacked," she replied.

"That's maybe all the more reason to talk," Don said.

"No," said Gloria after a thoughtful pause. "It just wouldn't be the right thing to do. I just don't think it would work out well."

It is possible to criticize Gloria for not being willing to deal face-to-face with Pastor Nathan. On the other hand, Pastor Nathan, as a church leader and leader of this Bible class, was not behaving in ways that facilitated open conversation. He was not providing a place of relative safety, and in fact was facilitating an unsafe place because he was aggressively disagreeing with the participants in the class. He was actively attacking the people who spoke up by suggesting that they were misinformed and not knowledgeable. Disagreement would actually be expected in learning situations like this; class participants need the opportunity to wrestle with the meaning of a text, and in that wrestling, they begin to apply it to their lives.

In addition to disagreeing and attacking, Pastor Nathan went on the defensive: "He reminded us that . . . he was the expert in the room." In this context, people are likely to protect themselves from attack. Bible class was rapidly becoming an unsafe experience. The result was increasing mistrust and decreasing class participation.

Patrick Lencioni puts it this way: "The first dysfunction [of a team] is an absence of trust among team members. Essentially, this stems from their unwillingness to be vulnerable within the group."[35]

---

35 Lencioni, *Overcoming the Five Dysfunctions of a Team*, 188.

So we learn things like, "look out for number one" or "don't let 'em see you sweat" or whatever other cliché calls for us to think of ourselves before others. And while this may be wise counsel if you're in prison, on a team it's lethal. The key to all of this, then, is to teach team members to get comfortable being exposed to one another, unafraid to honestly say things like "I was wrong" and "I made a mistake" and "I need help" and "I'm not sure" and "you're better at this than I am at that" and yes, even "I'm sorry." If team members cannot bring themselves to readily speak these words when the situation calls for it, they aren't going to learn to trust one another. Instead, they're going to waste time and energy thinking about what they *should* say, and wondering about the true intentions of their peers.[36]

While Lencioni writes from a business-leadership perspective, its applicability to human relationships and congregational dynamics is direct and clear. It is a basic task of church leaders to behave in ways that foster safety and trust within relationships and groups. There are three necessary ingredients to that.

1. Church leaders consistently behave in trustworthy ways. (See chapter 4.)

2. Church leaders share personal vulnerability. This is a risk, since there is no guarantee that such vulnerability will be respectfully engaged, even though within the Body of Christ it should be. (See also chapter 8.)

3. Church leaders facilitate the vulnerability of others in the group with a leadership style that encourages personal sharing and protects group members from attacks. Disagreement is expected; personal attack is not appropriate. In a group that is relatively trustworthy, and is, therefore, a relatively safe space, the dynamics of the group itself encourage participation and talking.

---

36 Lencioni, *Overcoming the Five Dysfunctions of a Team*, 18.

Safe spaces never occur by church leaders declaring, "This is a safe space. We want to get everyone's opinion about this." Anyone can assert such a thing, but behavior will almost always trump the spoken word. If church leaders assert that a group is a safe space, there must be an ongoing process continually demonstrating that it is so.

In safe spaces, there is room for differences and for vulnerability to be shared openly. Differences take on many forms. They may be evidenced in an idea about a building program that is inconsistent with those of the building committee, in the vulnerable feelings in response to the leadership style of the church leader, or in a church member's preoccupation with a conflict she is having with her teenage son. The differences are myriad, but all are opportunities for communication.

All differences are personal. They are vulnerabilities caused by opposing viewpoints—things people know about themselves (thoughts, feelings, experiences) that others might not know. But any difference will assuredly influence participation in the group. The safer the space the group creates, the more likely personal vulnerabilities will be shared. The more vulnerabilities are shared, the more useful and healthier they are. Safe and trusted space is modeled by and facilitated by the church leader.

Open communication within the group is at the core of a safe space, and often there is not enough of it. Corporate prayer connects vulnerabilities and differences to direct communication with God; safe spaces in the Body of Christ are generously sprinkled with prayer.

Jane, the new chair of the religious education committee, asked Frank to prepare the opening and closing devotions. She asked him to focus on the presence of Christ and the promise of the Holy Spirit's blessings at the beginning of the meeting and to summarize the concerns and activities of the meeting in prayer at its closing. In addition, she asked him to speak up and offer prayer in the midst of the meeting if there seemed to be a standstill or if people were not listening well or respecting one another's ideas or feelings.

None of those negative actions happened at the meeting, but something else did. Susan and Leon became very animated and upset as they talked about the decline of attendance at activities. Leon, close to tears, said, "I've been a member of this church for thirty-five years, and I remember it when it was really alive. And now I am heartbroken. I don't see young people. What's going to happen?"

Susan was more agitated: "Well, we've been meeting for several years and have never really gotten down to brass tacks. Discussion has been stifled. I'm really frustrated."

Frank intervened: "We've been discussing this for twenty minutes and have been increasingly open with one another about what we think and feel. This is what Jane is asking us to do. But sometimes we get into some raw feelings. Let's take a moment in silence, and then I'm going to offer a prayer." The group was silent for a few moments, then Frank prayed: "Dear Jesus, I praise You for the fulfillment of Your promise that where two or three are gathered, You are with them. So, You are with us. You see the task before us. You see and feel the pain of Leon and the frustration of Susan, and You see and feel the feelings of others in this room as well. Receive what we think and what we feel. Send Your Holy Spirit to help us use our feelings as well as our thoughts in ways that are useful to You. Continue to bless us, dear Jesus. Amen."

Donald Sloat suggests that there are four rules that, when followed, create all kinds of difficulties among communities of people who follow Christ. These rules are (1) don't trust, (2) don't talk, (3) don't feel, and (4) don't hope (want).[37] In the case of the religious education committee, Jane was beginning to encourage a healthier way: trust, talk, feel, and hope. Specifically, trust that each member will be respected and valued, talk so that each member knows what the other committee members are thinking, feel so that emotions are clearly identified and expressed, and hope so that a difference can be made and positive change can be made.

Pastor Nathan sensed that something was up, but he did not have words to express it. Attendance at his Bible class was going down. He was feeling more pressure to prepare and was aware that his speaking

---

37 Sloat, *Growing Up Holy and Wholly.* Sloat defines the four rules in chapter 9 (pp. 105–46) of his book and then discusses their behavioral implications in the chapters that follow.

was dominating the class. He tried a couple of times to ask for discussion, but people just avoided eye contact and looked at their Bibles.

It was hard for him to acknowledge, but he knew he needed help. There was a more experienced pastor, Pastor Francis, about twenty-five miles away. He liked this pastor and thought a conversation with him might be helpful.

It took almost an hour of discussion for Pastor Nathan to remember the personal put-downs he had made to class members and to connect those put-downs with some of his distress about the class. He knew he needed to talk about it with his colleague. The whole thing was pretty embarrassing. Pastor Francis, an empathic and insightful man, affirmed Pastor Nathan's skill and competence, but also underlined the destructiveness that Pastor Nathan now recognized was inherent in his responses.

When Pastor Francis asked Pastor Nathan what his next steps might be now that he recognized this, Pastor Nathan said softly, "I recognize this behavior, and I regret it. I am very sorry."

"Do you also want to say that aloud to Jesus?" asked Pastor Francis.

"Yes, will you hear my confession?" responded Pastor Nathan. Pastor Nathan spoke deeply of his disrespect of the Bible class members and of his personal attack on them, of his sorrow for what he now saw in his behavior—and of his repentance. Pastor Francis declared clearly and directly the forgiveness that is given by Christ, and absolution was given.

Freshly calmed and renewed by the gracious forgiveness of Christ offered in the context of an increasingly warm and rewarding relationship with Pastor Francis, Pastor Nathan continued: "I think I have some things to do. First, at the next Bible class meeting, I will specifically talk with the people who were involved and ask for their forgiveness as well."

Pastor Francis affirmed this next step and asked if Pastor Nathan would return so they could follow up. Pastor Nathan agreed.

It was not easy. But Pastor Nathan did what he said he would do. The three people who were directly involved all recognized what had happened between Pastor Nathan and each of them. They forgave him.

Following that, each initiated a discussion that had a similar theme: they had gone to others to share what had happened and criticized Pastor Nathan. They asked for his forgiveness, which he gave. And they resolved to tell others, especially those to whom they spoke, that this reconciliation had occurred.

Pastor Nathan continued to visit Pastor Francis once a month. He used the time to reflect on his ministry in general; his own defensiveness when challenged; and his experiences growing up, where he learned not to be vulnerable in front of his family. He also used the time for ongoing confession.

Gloria's jaw practically dropped the Sunday Pastor Nathan publicly apologized to members of the class. She could not wait to share this with Don, her husband. This positive word really spread. She became an active supporter of Pastor Nathan's ministry.

Building trust takes personal vulnerability. The process of building trust takes time and is never completed, but many leaps forward can be taken when church leaders risk vulnerability. Moreover, the ongoing trust-building process needs to be redone and reaffirmed time after time. If Pastor Nathan returned to personal attack, for example, trust would again deteriorate because safety would again be challenged. If Bible class members agree to monitor this behavior in themselves and in one another, trust-building is easier to achieve and maintain.

Jane added one feature to the agenda of every meeting of the religious education committee: debriefing at the end of the meeting. The questions for the debriefing were general ones: What is your overall response to our work this evening? How are you feeling; that is, what emotions are you having as a result of our meeting? How do you think we are doing together? When she first instituted this, Jane intentionally did not offer her debrief first. So, when she explained what she was doing and what she hoped would happen, there was an uncomfortable silence. Frank thought it would be a good time to pray about it, but he had a quick second thought: "Why don't I just share my feelings and thoughts about our work together this evening?" And so he did. Over the months, debriefing became a regular agenda item. The expectation, which developed at the second meeting, was that every-one participated.

Dedicating time to debriefing after a meeting can also be a way that a church leader builds trust within a group. Doing so fosters communication about work together in the present context of the group's work. Feelings and thoughts are honored. *Trust, talk, feel*, and *hope* are encouraged and behaviorally practiced. A space that is safer and safer forms.

Speaking Personally

When I first came to the LCMS International Center as a staff person, a book showed up on my desk. To this day I do not know who put it there. It was Donald Sloat's *Growing Up Holy and Wholly: Understanding and Hope for Adult Children of Evangelicals*. His use of trust, talk, feel, and hope as important aspects of the life of the church community was refreshing and eye-opening for me. The rules "Don't trust, don't talk, don't feel, and don't hope" were all the rules in my family when I was growing up. I began to see how these "don'ts" fostered a significant gap between how folks like me were presenting ourselves: on the outside we were fine, but on the inside, other things were stirring. Soon after that, I met David Hilton, whose quotation is in this chapter. It became clearer to me that all of us were, among other things, in search of authentic relationships. Where might those relationships best be found? How about in the Body of Christ, where Jesus is totally authentic and absolutely our Redeemer! I encourage you to read Sloat's book. (He has another volume, *The Dangers of Growing Up in a Christian Home*.)

If my point is not yet clear, I will state it clearly now: trust and trustworthiness, in the context of relationships and groups of people, do not come easily to me. Safe spaces are important aspects of this. Sometimes I am slow to see them. However, the Holy Spirit works.

If you want more to read on this topic, I recommend Patrick Lencioni's *The Five Dysfunctions of a Team: A Leadership Fable* and *Overcoming the Five Dysfunctions of a Team: A Field Guide for Leaders*. Both are terrific and have been a tremendous help to me. If you appreciate the Lencioni books, then pick up *Death by Meeting*. It will reinforce this discussion.

CHAPTER EIGHT

Disclosure, Feedback, and Discovery

Liz walked through the door of her house at 10:15 p.m. after a three-hour meeting of the property committee, which she chaired. Frustrated, she slammed the door slightly harder than usual.

"Wow! That was quite a slam!" Silas shouted from the family room, with a touch of humor in his voice. He knew something was up.

"Don't criticize me. Just mind your own business," retorted Liz.

Silas, a little irritated, knew better than to respond in the midst of his irritation, so he took a minute to calm himself. He knew that Liz was frustrated about many things because of the building program going on at church. She had shared some of her feelings in their previous conversations together.

Liz knew she was edgy, so she went into the kitchen and made herself a cup of green tea. She came into the family room, where Silas was sitting. He got up and opened his arms to her. Liz put down the cup and hugged Silas.

"I'm sorry I yelled at you," said Liz. "The meeting just got to me tonight. It wasn't you."

Silas responded, "I know you're really struggling with this building project and sometimes get pretty frustrated. I am glad you've shared your feelings with me before and now. Let's talk some more. Thanks for *the apology. It is warmly and gratefully accepted. And I think I could have responded better to your coming in this evening as well. I know this is a tough time for you."*

"Thanks," Liz said. She and Silas sat together and talked for a half hour before they went to bed.

In order to effectively lead, church leaders do well to cultivate personal qualities that help them grow into being more aware of themselves and how their behaviors affect others. Three of these qualities are (1) capacity for self-disclosure and transparency, (2) openness to feedback from others, and (3) willingness to risk exploration into new territory, both in personal and in skill-development arenas. The Johari Window, a product of Joseph Luft and Harry Ingham in 1955, is a relatively easy model for a church leader to use to build these qualities.

One observation of the communication between Liz and Silas is that it took place in what is a relatively safe space for them. Liz has shared her frustration previously. As a result, Silas has a context in which to place her behavior. Liz has not kept her emotions inside; rather, she has shared them with Silas. When she has these feelings again and has an opportunity to express them, she can do so openly.

This communication is in the public area between Liz and Silas, where things that are known to one person are known to the other. This is the first window of the diagram pictured on the following page.

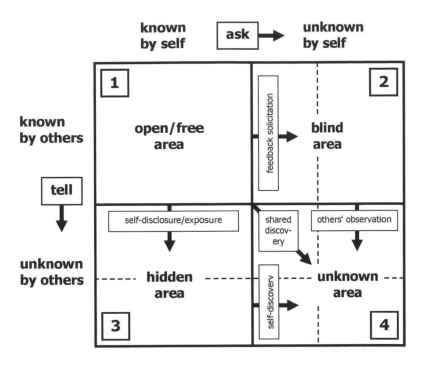

Johari Window[38]

The Johari Window operates along two dimensions: (1) known or unknown to self, and (2) known or unknown to others. This is a relatively simple way to think about human relationships because it places thoughts and feelings into four simple quadrants. For instance, if a person is angry and suppressing it, the anger may affect how that person behaves and even what that person does. That anger could be "known to others, unknown to self." The anger could be known to the individual, but disguised well enough that it is not known to others: "known to self, unknown to others." It could be unknown to both the person and to others. That is, neither the individual nor others are aware of the underlying emotion: "unknown to self, unknown to others." Finally, the anger

---

38 The Johari Window was originally published by Luft, J., and Ingham, H. in *The Johari Window: A Graphic Model for Interpersonal Relations* (Los Angeles: University of California Western Training Lab, 1955).

could be known to the person as well as to others. This is the "known to self, known to others" window, in which Silas and Liz were operating.

The "known to self, known to others" window is where human relationships can thrive. It is where healthy relationships contribute to the effective and efficient completion of tasks. Here, more of the inner world of thoughts and feelings of one person is shared with another person or with a group, and the sharing is done mutually. People learn more about one another, relationships deepen, and tasks are more readily dealt with. People are not confused, unsure, or doubtful concerning the feelings, thoughts, or actions of others.

One of the ways that church leaders can lead is to facilitate and encourage the community to move more of their communications into the "known to self, known to others" category. This serves to strengthen relationships and give them energy to grow. The facilitation and encouragement to enlarge the "known to self, known to others" window is not done primarily by verbal encouragement, although that may certainly be part of it. Enlarging this window is most effective when it combines verbal and nonverbal behavior.

In order to have an expanding "known to self, known to others" window, the church leaders will be actively working to develop the following attitudes, skills, and behaviors: encouragement of feedback; sharing of personal vulnerability; and engagement of curiosity, discovery, and exploration.

The following examples will highlight these characteristics as representative of activity in each of the Johari Window quadrants.

A director of Christian education, Janice has been in her current position for a year and a half. As she reflected on her work, things looked like they were going quite well. The involvement of the youth of the parish had increased, as had the number of youth participating. She was welcomed by almost everyone in the congregation in a friendly way. But when she went to the church council meeting, she thought that the interactions she had with other council members were pretty businesslike and matter-of-fact.

Janice was outgoing and vivacious, and she had grown up in a family that was prone to outward display of feelings, especially warm ones, and a general acceptance of almost all feelings. There was an exception, though: when her parents were either disappointed or irritated with her. At those times, her parents withdrew from her somewhat and were silent. Those moments made her wonder whether her parents still really loved her, although deep down, she knew that they did because they would eventually say so and behave consistently with that.

The church council meetings brought back these kinds of memories in very small ways. She was especially concerned about the chairman, Alec, and Louise, the council member Janice worked with most because her position fell within Louise's area of oversight.

For Janice, emotionally it came down to whether they liked her, and she was not at all sure. Adding to her uncertainty, the council did not conduct formal performance evaluations of the church and school staff, so Janice had never been evaluated.

After the last council meeting, Janice approached Louise and said, "Louise, I'd like to sit with you and Alec, if possible, to discuss how you view my work here and how you view me. We've not had that conversation, and I would like us to have it."

Louise was surprised at Janice's request since she thought Janice knew how much the overwhelming majority of the congregation liked her and how appreciative people were of her work. But she also respected Janice and sensed that this was important to her.

"Let's do it. I'll talk to Alec, and we'll set up a meeting. How about you put into words a few sentences about what you'd like the meeting to focus on. Send that to us before the meeting so we'll be more prepared. I hear so far that you want to discuss what we see in you and your work here. Expand on that, just briefly."

Janice left knowing that she had taken an important step. She could not read well the responses of these church leaders to her, and she had initiated a way to find out.

Janice was using the skill of getting feedback. She had increasing anxiety because there were things "known to others, but not known to self" that were concerning her. It was the blind space that was precipitating her anxiety. In that blind space, Janice was drawing on meaning that came from her family of origin. The way to find out whether her projection into the unknown window was accurate was to ask for feedback. This is what she did. In doing so, both Louise and Alec were able to discuss how pleased members of the congregation were with her work and how much they liked her.

It takes considerable courage to be as direct as Janice was about asking for feedback. There is risk involved. But how else can church leaders expand the "known to the self, known to others" window to more aspects of their lives? Performance evaluations are formal ways to do this, which helps to relieve some of the burden of having to ask for feedback. Teachers may give students grades that move a teacher's opinion about a student's work to the "open" window. Pastors may have feedback groups to solicit sermon feedback. Meeting facilitators or chairpersons may ask attendees to share what may be unknown to other members of the committee: "What is your overall response, thinking, and feeling to our meeting today?"

Requesting feedback takes courage and confidence. The best context for this is relatively safe relationships. Requesting and receiving feedback is a vital skill of a church leader. It moves more of the relationship dynamics into the known area.

Bill, the director of Christian outreach at his congregation, was riding high, as he led very successful outreach initiatives. In just three months, congregation members had contacted more than two hundred people who had no church affiliation, and over twenty of those people were now worshiping regularly and enrolled in new-member classes. Bill was extremely popular within the congregation and used his naturally bubbly personality very effectively.

But life at home was very different and much darker than the positive light in which most people saw him. When he came home, he would have dinner with his spouse and children and then retreat to his man cave. There he would plunge into the darkness of exhaustion, despair, and depression. His wife, Mary, tried to talk to him about seeking help, but he refused.

At first, Mary was not willing to ask Bill to seek help because she believed that if the congregation found out about it, Bill would lose his job. Then what would they do? But as the situation became more desperate, Mary became more insistent. Finally, Bill consented to consult a counselor.

After several months in counseling, of exercise, and of taking medication, Bill was improving. He decided to approach one member of the congregation's worker support team (WST). [This WST concept has been more fully described in my book Holding Up the Prophet's Hand.] To Bill's surprise, Sherri, the WST member, was fully supportive of him and the steps he had taken. She and he decided to talk together with the whole WST, which was equally supportive. Bill decided to add their pastor to those who knew of his situation. The pastor met with Bill monthly to discuss his spiritual life, in addition to his counseling.

Three years later, Bill began teaching a class for the congregation on struggles and recovery. He called it "My Experience with Depression." Several months later, he offered the class again for the congregation and the community. In both cases, attendance was exceptional.

Bill learned to use the skill of sharing. At first, he strove to keep his dark pain secret, managing it as though the community of the Body of Christ was more or less an enemy. Later, buoyed by his sharing, he found the community of the Body of Christ to be supportive and helpful. In order for the community to know what he was struggling with, he needed to share the struggle. Happily, the community knew how to be supportive of him.

This is the third of the four Johari Windows: "known to self but not known to others." It forms the gap between that which persons know about themselves and that which others know about them. Generally, the less of a gap there is, the closer the relationship is; the wider the gap, the more distant the relationship. Self-disclosure requires relationships that are more safe and welcoming of such information sharing.

There are levels of personal sharing. No one knows everything about someone else. Nor should they. But effective church leaders have the capacity for genuine, personal revelation. By doing so, church leaders encourage others to do the same. In order to weep when others weep and rejoice when others rejoice (see Romans 12:15), it is necessary to know of the weeping and the rejoicing that is occurring. In order to pray for another, it is necessary to know at least something of the content of the prayer to be prayed.

Thus, church leaders are not focused solely on church business in their relationships with others. They are also concerned about and responsive to the personal side of all relationships. An active and vibrant interplay occurs between the necessary work to be done and the realities of personal life and context. This is why working together so often helps relationships develop, as people attend to a task but also have opportunity to share about themselves. In so doing, "known to self, known to others" increases. The skill required for this is personal sharing and vulnerability.

As Janice requested and received feedback on concerns that were important to her, and as Bill shared more about his struggle and received support and encouragement, their Johari Window would look more like the one on the following page.

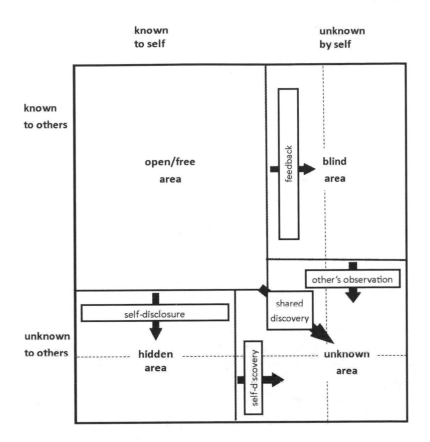

Johari Window 2: "Unknown by self, unknown to others"

"Here it is, coming up to Thanksgiving again," reflected Lisa. "Every year, it is the same thing: when November begins, I start going downhill emotionally. It is little by little, but by the time Thanksgiving rolls around, I know I want to be, am supposed to be, and would like to be happy. My brother and sister-in-law come over for Thanksgiving, or we go to their house. The cousins get along well and the tradition we've established is pretty terrific. But I just can't get into it. It affects my work too, because I have less energy and can't concentrate."

Lisa's husband, Mark, had noticed this for the seven years they had been married and even in the two years they dated. In this, the ninth year he had known Lisa, he asked, "Are you starting to feel like you usually feel about this time of year?"

The question was a welcome one to Lisa. "I am."

"Do you have any idea what this is about?"

"No," Lisa said.

"Maybe," Mark mused, "since this happens every year, you or the both of us could go talk to someone find out why."

"Maybe," Lisa replied.

Their conversation turned into a call to a local counselor, where Lisa made an appointment for herself. She entered the office of her soon-to-be-counselor, was warmly greeted, and they both sat down.

"What brings you in?" asked the counselor.

Lisa explained the reason she was there, describing the repetition of these depressed feelings around this time of year.

Her counselor, after being sure she understood Lisa's situation and that Lisa wanted to get to the bottom of it, asked, "Do you have any idea what might be causing or influencing this?"

"The best I can think of," answered Lisa, "is that it is fall; all the leaves are coming off the trees and winter is coming. Things look almost dead."

"You see less vibrant life around you, and in some way that disturbs you," reflected the counselor. "Think for a moment," continued the counselor. "Was there anything that happened around this time of year that changed for you, like the seasons changing, that made life darker and less alive-looking?"

Tears began to form in Lisa's eyes and soon became a flood of weeping. "My mom. My mom died on November 21 when I was seventeen."

Lisa spent the next several months in counseling, working through the impact of her mother's death on her and the emotions connected with it. Lisa had had to be strong for her dad and her younger brother. Her family did not talk very much about emotions, and although strong emotions were involved, they did not surface in a way that could be processed well. Lisa buried her grief inside herself, but it still *affected her. The connection between her mom's death and her seasonal depression, though obvious when the story is told, was buried deep inside herself.*

Lisa's story is an example of "unknown by self, unknown to others." Here, there were both feelings and information connected to a past event that was influencing the present, but the connection was not consciously known to her and was also unknown to others. Lisa's increased depression was known by her and by Mark. Her emotional state was in the open window between her and Mark. Mark was free to ask for feedback to check out his perception of Lisa. Lisa was free to share that his observations were accurate. But neither could go further. Mark's suggestion to Lisa and her acceptance of that suggestion led her to a place where discovery could take place. Her counselor would not immediately know of the connection until Lisa provided information. As that information was shared, her counselor asked about Lisa's history, and the connection emerged and quickly moved to the open area where it could be addressed. The months following would explore all three windows: where the counselor offered feedback; where Lisa shared more information, memories, and feelings; and where connections were discovered. All this led to an expansion of "known to self, known to others."

These capacities—personal sharing and vulnerability, openness to feedback, and search for discovery—are not easy capacities to enact. But it is clear that church leaders who lead from a "known to self, known to others" perspective are more likely to help others behave in similar ways. Disclosure should always occur in a pattern and at a pace that is relatively comfortable for people, although discomfort in sharing should not always be the reason to stop sharing. Sometimes discomfort is necessary to facilitate trust. Feedback always should be given with care and empathy. Self-discovery always presents opportunity for growth.

All of these situations require courage in church leaders that is not just of a personal kind. Such courage is born of the Holy Spirit and is gifted by that same Spirit, as it is done for the purpose of and in the context of building up the Body of Christ.

Speaking Personally

I am much more receptive to feedback when I believe that the person who is offering it is interested in my well-being and best interests.

In my junior year of high school, I took up pipe smoking. It was "in" to smoke, but I really hated cigarettes. Nevertheless, I felt like I needed to conform, so I got a pipe. Through the remainder of high school, through college and graduate school, after I married and began raising a family, I continued to smoke a pipe. In fact, one of my pleasant memories is of our two sons in the back of the car, competing for the chance to put tobacco into my pipe.

Our sons were going into the eighth and tenth grades when we moved from Chicago to Syracuse, New York. Both of them had health classes in their new school. Right after Christmas, our conversation turned to my pipe. I do not remember their precise language, but it was something like, "Dad, you have taught us to pay attention to what we put into our bodies, but we are learning that you are putting bad stuff into your body when you are smoking."

In Johari language, our sons were sharing something they were thinking (known to them but unknown to me). They risked moving it into the "known to self, known to others" area by offering feedback. As the conversation proceeded, it became clear that they wanted me to stop smoking. I felt defensive, but it was clear they had my best interests at heart. I knew that I should quit, and I did. But it was not easy. I still long for a pipe after a good meal, but I have not smoked since that conversation more than thirty years ago.

Using the Johari Window is easy. You can find more information about it on www.businessballs.com, which is especially useful, as are www.mindtools.com and www.humanresourcefulness.net. Congregational life, I am convinced, would be considerably strengthened if church leaders intentionally developed capacities for disclosure and transparency, openness to feedback, and willingness to explore new personal and skill arenas.

CHAPTER NINE

Outside Influences

"I just don't know what the trouble is," Jim, the congregational president, said to his wife, Lydia. "I feel like there is a barrier between me and Pastor Carl that I can't get over. He seems so distant, and we are not clicking together. He does not seem as caring as, well, Pastor Fred was. I'm wondering if maybe we actually called the wrong guy. But on the other hand, maybe it's me. Got any ideas?"

Lydia smiled and put her hand on Jim's as she said, "You know, you and Pastor Fred worked closely together for the last decade as you were an elder and then the president of the congregation. Besides that, you had a great and warm personal relationship. It's been two years since Pastor Fred took another call. You were pretty downcast about that. It was like you lost a close friend. I mean, it really was that you lost a close friend and your pastor as well. Maybe you are still saddened by Pastor Fred's leaving, and that is making it hard to get over the barrier you experience between you and Pastor Carl."

Jim's eyes moistened. "I think you've got something," he said.

No one comes to a conversation or a relationship as a blank slate. All people have histories that inform their present life and relationships. At times, those histories help strengthen a relationship; at other times they inhibit it. Church leaders recognize when their current leadership, interaction with others, and general attitudes are influenced by past experiences and by their own past behavioral patterns brought into the present.

What might be the history behind some of Jim's response to Pastor Carl? Indeed, it may be that Pastor Carl's personality style is a bit more reserved than the previous pastor's. It may be, therefore, that Jim's task is to explore the nature of his experience with others who have kept him at arm's length.

But even if Jim's concerns are caused by Pastor Carl's personality style in contrast to Pastor Fred's, there is clearly another factor, suggested by Lydia, that provokes Jim's emotional response: has he worked through his grief at Pastor Fred's leaving to the extent that he has the emotional energy to work at engaging Pastor Carl? When Pastor Fred left, Jim lost both a close friend and a pastor. This was a very meaningful relationship for Jim on a number of different levels because they had worked together in church administration and ministry matters and had become close friends. Could it be that some (or even most) of Jim's difficulties with Pastor Carl have to do with unresolved grief over the loss of Pastor Fred?

Dealing with this kind of loss is a real challenge for everyone, but especially for church leaders. From a positive aspect, Jim is looking at all relationships as mutually created and, therefore, as mutually satisfying. From the negative angle, which is Jim's perspective in this circumstance, a previous relationship that was very good may cause a church leader to feel resentment at the change. Then, the church leader must resist the temptation to ascribe a problem or negative characteristic to the new staff member, to defend himself or herself by pointing out a negative trait as a reason for a difficult circumstance, or to view himself or herself as innocent or passive in the new dynamic. Therefore, it is imperative that each party look at his or her own participation in making the relationship what it is. In order to do that, church leaders must consider the possibility that at least part of the problem may be themselves.

Instead of deciding that the barrier to relationship is of Pastor Carl's making exclusively, Jim comes to consider that he is likely contributing to what is happening. In Jim's case, it could be unresolved grief.

But Pastor Carl did, of course, have a part in all this, as did the former pastor, Pastor Fred.

Chuck, an older member of the congregation who had given Jim counsel on several occasions in his life, had become a close friend of Jim's over the years. One day, he received a call from Jim: "I'd like to talk to you about an important spiritual concern I have. Could I come and talk in the next day or so?" And so they talked. As it turned out, Chuck was also sad at the loss of Pastor Fred, and the two of them openly shared their sadness with each other.

"I knew this was the God-pleasing and right thing for Pastor Fred to do," Jim said. "His new congregation needs the gifts and talents he brings, and needs them badly. It also allows Pastor Fred and his family to move closer to his aging parents, something that I know is very important for him. It was a good thing; I still didn't like it."

The conversation lasted for a little over an hour. At the end of the conversation, Chuck had an idea: "I don't know about you, Jim, but I did not talk clearly to Pastor Fred about my thoughts and feelings about his leaving; we just didn't get to that level. How about calling him up and telling him about this conversation and how we are still grieving his departure?" They prayed together about this. Jim, Chuck, and Pastor Fred had the conversation the following week.

After the conversation with Pastor Fred, Jim and Chuck got together again to debrief the conversation and to discuss where each of them was in their dealing with the change. Chuck admitted that he was not experiencing the same distance that Jim was with Pastor Carl.

"I believe," Jim said thoughtfully, "that I will call Pastor Carl and ask to meet with him. Perhaps he has been feeling some of the distance from me that I have with him and we can work through it. Even if he doesn't feel the same way, I will talk to him about what I have been going through." And so they talked.

In the course of their conversation, Pastor Carl said, "You know, Jim, I've sensed a bit of the distance, and I haven't quite known what to make of it. But now I have some history that helps me better understand you and what is happening. But I must confess to you that it is not all you. I have heard from others what kind of a warm and interactive person Pastor Fred was during his time here. He seemed to be very outgoing, caring, and, as they say, extroverted. I am a pretty caring person too, but I am more reserved and less extroverted than he seems to have been. I am working on this. But because I am more of an introvert, I want you to know that I am no less caring. Let's agree to come back to this from time to time. Specifically, let's meet about three or four months from now, so we can come back to the question of this distance between us."

This conversation ended with both men praying in thanksgiving and also for the Holy Spirit's work to strengthen their relationship.

Here are the fruits of this growing relationship:

- Mutual accountability for the nature of the relationship

- Personal responsibility for one's interpersonal characteristics

- Prayer for the Holy Spirit's power to build up a relationship in the Body of Christ

- Agreement to continue to process the nature of the relationship

- Awareness of how previous life circumstances influence present behaviors and attitudes

These fruits need ongoing cultivation to thrive. The relationship between Jim and Pastor Carl would not have been cultivated at all if Jim had left his concerns unspoken ("known to self, unknown to others") or if Pastor Carl had become defensive about his introversion. The relationship would not have been cultivated if Jim blamed or attacked Pastor Carl or if Pastor Carl failed to recognize that both parties create relationship dynamics. Together, Pastor Carl and Jim are forging a stronger relationship.

Principal Cheryl was pretty downcast following the latest faculty meeting. All signs were pointing to a continuing forward movement of the school, including small increases in enrollment. Finances were stable. Each faculty member seemed to be doing his or her job well, as far as she could see. But there was something, she thought, that was not clicking when they met together. There were conflicts between the faculty members and, while the business of the faculty was getting done, there was almost always some negative response. The responses were not particularly helpful and did nothing to clarify what the group was discussing. Rather, faculty members' remarks had the tone of ongoing irritability or, perhaps, of emotional shortness.

As she continued to mull this over, Cheryl had an opportunity to consult with another principal, Joyce, who offered the following advice: "Perhaps there are things going on in the lives of some of the faculty members that have them on edge. Maybe if they had a chance to share that, it would be helpful both to them and to the group as a whole."

Principal Cheryl wondered about that for a moment and remembered something that happened regularly in her small-group Bible study. At the beginning of each study session, every member was offered an opportunity to bring forward a prayer request.

This gave Cheryl an idea: "I think I'll do that," she mused. "At the beginning of every meeting, I'll ask if there are things for which we should pray."

"Great idea," said Joyce.

And so she did. At the next faculty meeting, Principal Cheryl introduced what she was going to do very simply: "As we open our meeting, rejoicing in the fulfillment of Jesus' promise to be among us and praying for the Holy Spirit to bless our work and our conversation, I want to include in our prayers things that are on each of our hearts. Please share what you'd like us to pray for."

Silence. Faculty members looked around a bit nervously. Cheryl had expected some hesitation since such a practice was new and was not necessarily part of the ongoing experience of the faculty at its meetings. She looked around, making as much eye contact as possible.

"I will begin," Principal Cheryl spoke softly. "My mom has just been diagnosed with skin cancer. She will have surgery to remove several cancerous growths the day after tomorrow. The doctor says everything will be all right, and my mom thinks so as well. But she is *understandably anxious, and I am upset too. I'd like us to pray for my mom, her surgery, and for healing."*

Quiet. But it was a different kind of quiet—not as nervous as before.

"I have something," said Kate, the third-grade teacher. "Now that my son is in high school, he is struggling with his grades. He is unhappy, and I want to help him, but he really . . . well, he really seems like he doesn't want my help. I'd appreciate it if we could pray for him and for me as well."

Slowly, several other faculty members (not everyone) spoke up. All spoke of some concern they had and how they needed and wanted prayer. Prayers were offered for all. This prayer time took about twenty minutes of the faculty meeting, but that did not seem to matter. The remaining faculty business was concluded relatively quickly, and, while there were differences of opinion about some of the agenda items, the tone of the conversation and the meeting overall was different.

"Perhaps we could begin our meetings like this, at least for a while," Principal Cheryl suggested. Almost everyone agreed.

Here are the backbones of these growing relationships:

- Church leadership that both invites and participates in personal sharing
- Recognizing the presence of Christ in the gathering of the community of His followers
- Praying for the Holy Spirit's blessing to build relationships in the Body of Christ
- Setting aside time for sharing and praying
- Preparing for the possibility that there will not be immediate and energetic responses at the beginning
- Committing to the process of sharing and praying
- Awareness that outside-life circumstances influence present behavior

All church leaders have decisions to make about their leadership style along the attention to task/attention to person axis. Both ends of the axis are important. Focusing too much toward the personal side can make accomplishing tasks less efficient. Focusing too much toward the task side may decrease creativity and efficiency because it does not consider that people come to meetings and roles with their whole person. Despite their best efforts, it is hard for people to compartmentalize their lives in such a way that one part does not affect another. In this case, outside-of-the-room concerns can get in the way of conducting the business at hand. Taking the time to inquire about prayer needs allowed outside influences to be placed on the inside table, which resulted in a strengthening of relationships.

Alex's blood pressure was soaring and his heart was racing. He was in a meeting of the education committee of his congregation, and members of the committee were evaluating his performance. Alex was just a few years into his vocation as director of Christian education, and he loved his job. At the moment, everyone in the meeting was in agreement that he was a very likable and energetic young man who was easy to get along with and who connected very well with the young people in the congregation. This was an important area of his responsibility, and the members of the committee saw that he was on the same wavelength as the youth. Plaudits were shared all around.

That is where Alex thought the evaluation should have stopped. But unfortunately, from his point of view, there was another area of his responsibility that was not going so well, at least as the members of the committee were discussing presently: his development of Bible studies for the adults of the congregation.

"You do not seem to have the kind of connection with middle-aged adults and older individuals that you have with the youth of the congregation," observed the chair of the committee, Jeff, himself a forty-six-year-old father of a college-age son and two teenage daughters.

"He sounds just like my dad," raged DCE Alex inside. "I was never good enough. There were things he praised, but he always found something wrong as well."

Alex tried to keep his composure, but he had heard this kind of feedback before from other congregation members. "Why can't they just see what I'm good at?" he asked himself.

"Alex, this conversation seems to be upsetting to you now," Jeff said. "Let's break for a brief prayer about this. Dear Jesus, You are present in our midst and You see that our conversation together is getting a bit heated. Send Your Holy Spirit to bless our conversation, even in the midst of the frustration that is evident in my brother-in-You Alex, and in me, and perhaps in others. Calm us and bless our heartfelt conversation. Amen."

The prayer and the empathy Alex felt worked to calm his thoughts and decrease his blood pressure. The break time continued as everyone refilled their water, tea, or coffee containers, and Alex worked to frame a response. He really liked the members of the committee and respected Jeff a lot. He admitted that he struggled with his work with the older members of the congregation, but he was not convinced he could be as honest with them as he wanted to be. Jeff also felt calmer and wondered how he could foster a better relationship with Alex.

As the committee reassembled, Jeff began: "I'd like to find ways to work better together on this, Alex. We aren't connecting well. I am sure both of us are making this so. But I want you to know that I want this relationship to work well. How can I help it get stronger?"

This was an invitation that Alex could never remember hearing. Perhaps it had come before from Jeff or even from his dad when he was younger, but he did not think so. Somehow this invitation made a difference. "You are on to a struggle I have," Alex hesitantly began. "I struggle with being criticized because it says to me that I am not good enough, and I want very much to be good enough."

Alex was surprised when several committee members shared that they had had similar struggles, and by the end of the meeting, he felt just a little more that he was a partner with the committee rather than an antagonist. "There is lots more work to be done," he said to himself as he drove home after the meeting. "I have heard our pastor talk about counseling as being helpful, and our health insurance plan has good benefits. Maybe it's time that I took a better look at this and how it fits into to my relationship with my dad."

Here are the backbones of these growing relationships:

- Church leadership that both invites personal sharing and participates in it

- Recognition of the presence of Christ in the gathering of the community of His followers

- Prayer for the Holy Spirit to address the specific emotions that were being felt, not just in the identified person (i.e., Alex), but also in others

- Direct addressing of the emotional concerns

- Utilization of prayer and time out to give opportunity for a calming to occur

- Invitation to join a partnering relationship, as opposed to an adversarial one

- Awareness that life history in relationships influences the way relationships are handled in the present

Here, Alex's openness and capacity to receive feedback (eventually) move him to consider counseling. This is often appropriate when unresolved aspects of one's life history interfere with present functioning.

These three vignettes reinforce the notion that all of us come to relationships and tasks with our present context of concerns, joys, and challenges, and with our life history. These can have positive influences and aid in the building up of relationships in the Body of Christ, or they can have negative influences as they cause a darker turn in relationships.

Church leaders recognize that this is so and work to constructively and positively address these influences, not only in others but in themselves as well. If church leaders address only these influences in others and not in themselves, they risk behaving in less helpful ways. If they do not see the mutual causality in the relationship and blame the other person for the problem, the barrier to relationship may increase. Awareness of both self and others must be present.

Speaking Personally

Join me in considering how often one relationship is influenced by outside "stuff." My list is long, but here is one example from my early counseling training experience:

I was beginning to learn how to do marital counseling. One of the first couples that came to me was a highly conflicted, angry-at-each-other-and-saying-so-at-every-opportunity couple. The session was a disaster, and, of course, they did not return. Why should they? Why pay to do to each other what they could do for free? As I discussed my experience with my supervisor, he asked, "What did this remind you of?"

My response came quickly: "Growing up." My parents fought a lot, and I was, for the most part, able to calm them down by talking about something I had done. In other words, my strategy was to move my parents' conversation toward me and away from their conflict with each other. (Not that I was consciously aware of that strategy at the time!) The outside influence was my own past experience, and that affected my capacity to do my work effectively, to say the least. I was, experientially, back at home in the room with the couple who had come to me.

This is how outside influences can work. It often takes conversation to sort it out, but that's just what we as church leaders must do.

CHAPTER TEN

The Brain

Everyone has a brain. Understanding how it works is important. Brain research is expanding and will continue to revolutionize our understanding of the person. Church leaders who wish to understand more about the self and the flock can use this emerging research to build up the Body of Christ.

In the last few years, many emphases on brain study have been published. On July 17, 1990, then-President George H. W. Bush proclaimed 1990 to be the beginning of the "Decade of the Brain":

> The human brain, a 3-pound mass of interwoven nerve cells that controls our activity, is one of the most magnificent—and mysterious—wonders of creation. The seat of human intelligence, interpreter of senses, and controller of movement, this incredible organ continues to intrigue scientists and layman alike.[39]

In April 2013, President Barack Obama announced a $100 million program, and then matched that amount in 2015:

> The Brain Research through Advancing Innovative Neurotechnologies (BRAIN) Initiative is part of a Presidential

---

39 "Presidential Proclamation 6158," Library of Congress, accessed July 27, 2015, loc.gov/loc/brain/proclaim.HTML.

focus aimed at revolutionizing our understanding of the human brain. By accelerating the development and application of innovative technologies, researchers will be able to produce a revolutionary new dynamic picture of the brain that, for the first time, shows how individual cells and complex neural circuits interact in both time and space.[40]

The Year of the Brain—Europe was announced in 2015 with the following:

Understanding the human brain and the diseases that can affect it is one of the greatest scientific and philosophical challenges we face today.[41]

On the topic of brain research, I recently reviewed the book *Sticky Learning* by Holly J. Inglis:

Brain research is front and center, much research is being done and much writing is coming forth. Using this brain research for the good of the church would seem to be a self-evident task.[42]

There are two basic features that have been known for some time about the brain and its functions. The first is illustrated in the drawing that follows.

More than sixty years ago (1952), Paul MacLean of the National Institute of Mental Health, in Washington DC, developed an elegant and simple picture of the brain, calling it a triune brain. This interpretation has been used since as a meaningful way to describe some of the basic brain features.

---

40 "The BRAIN Initiative," The White House, accessed July 27, 2015, www.whitehouse.gov/BRAIN.

41 "The Year of the Brain," European Brain Council, accessed July 27, 2015, www.europeanbraincouncil.org/year-of-the-brain.

42 Bruce M. Hartung, review of *Sticky Learning: How Neuroscience Supports Teaching That's Remembered*, by Holly J. Inglis, *Concordia Journal* 41, no. 4 (Fall 2015): 364–65.

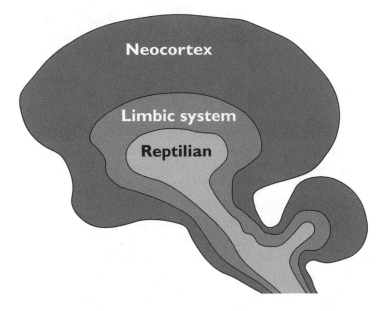

The R-complex is a part of the brain that humans share with all of God's creatures. It is the action-without-thinking section of the brain that communicates concerning issues of survival and pain. When a person is "downshifted" into this dominant R-complex area of motivation, empathic connection to others, thoughtful engagement of ideas, and processing of emotions do not happen. Behavior is instinctual, responses are automatic.

The limbic system controls chemical responses that lead to the experience of emotions; it is the place for the generation and regulation of emotions. For example, empathy, the capacity to sense what others are feeling, is generated here. Language is more rudimentary because it is not always clear to the person what words define what is being felt. Longer-term memory resides here as well, so emotions are connected to memory and determine how a person responds to specific circumstances. For instance, if a contemporary interaction between one person and another is similar to a previous interaction housed in the long-term memory and connected to negative feelings, the contemporary interaction will be doused with those long-ago bodily reactions. Learning does occur here, but not efficiently, because emotions, which are not stable, can interfere. In order to process emotions, the limbic system links to the third area, the cerebral cortex.

The cerebral cortex (also called the neocortex) is where higher order thinking, reasoning, problem solving, planning, looking ahead, creativity, and learning occur. Sometimes, it is referred to as the executive center. Dr. Paul MacLean called this area of the brain the place where the "mother of invention and the father of abstract thought" live. The best learning occurs here. In order to learn, however, there must be freedom from survival issues communicated by the R-complex and negative emotional signals from the limbic system. Both of these other systems will create a barrier to excellent cerebral cortex functioning. The disadvantage that the cerebral cortex has is that it is the slowest of the three brain sections. This means that the move to action without thinking (R-complex) or emotional reactivity (limbic system) will register more quickly than in the higher-order thinking cerebral cortex. Thus, a person can figuratively be hijacked by either of these systems.

Karen, secretary of the congregation's women's organization, was known as a mild-mannered and gracious fifty-one-year-old woman. It was no wonder, then, that her friends were shocked by her reaction when a car abruptly changed lanes in front of her as they were driving on the expressway at sixty-five miles per hour. Karen laid on the horn, yelled at the driver of the other car, sped up, passed the car, and cut off the driver. Then she said to her friends, "That will show him." When they arrived at the restaurant where they were having lunch, Karen said, "My goodness, I just don't know what got into me."

What got into Karen was the downshifting of her whole self when she was hijacked by her R-complex and her limbic system.

Twenty-two-year-old Gregory aspired to become a pastor and was encouraged to do so by just about everyone in his congregation. He frequently commented on social and religious issues that were posted on social media sites on the Internet. Most of his comments were one or two sentences and were generally laced with name-calling and invective language. A member of the congregation noticed this and, knowing of Gregory's interest in becoming a pastor, arranged a meeting with the pastor and Gregory together. He brought along some of the comments Gregory had posted on the Internet.

"When I see something that makes me angry, I just have to respond," Gregory explained. "I am sticking up for what I believe, and this is a free country with freedom of speech, after all."

Here, Gregory was using his cerebral cortex to rationalize, after the fact, his limbic system–motivated behavior, but his limbic system emotionality was really calling the shots.

It is important for church leaders to understand something of how the brain works. If the cerebral cortex is the slowest of the three parts of the brain, but the place where complex thinking and problem solving occur, then it is important to pause long enough for the cerebral cortex to catch up and take charge of the whole brain when faced with adversity. The task of church leaders is to have their whole brain functioning together under the dominance of the executive function. If the leader is caught up in R-complex or limbic system downshifting, then the people within the range of the leader's influence are likely to be caught up in the same processes.

General systems thinking tends to reinforce this concern from a group dynamics point of view. When groups become increasingly anxious— when they are more and more dominated by limbic system feelings and behavior, or, even more problematically, R-complex behavior—creative engagement in problem solving simply does not occur.

> When things are calmer, people are able to think more clearly about their options in the midst of stressful circumstances and develop a reasonable, workable plan of action. Effective leaders are able to help people manage their level of anxiety so they can accomplish these goals. They do this *primarily* by managing their own anxiety, and then, secondarily, by staying in meaningful contact with other key players in the situation. They do not tell others to "be calm." They simply bring their own calmness to the situation.[43]

---

43 Richardson, *Creating a Healthier Church*, 51.

There is also a process where the limbic system is blocked from connecting to the cerebral cortex in such a way that there is little emotional attachment or integration. When people say something like "We are all business," they usually mean that tasks are done with little emotional engagement. In such instances, there is no balance between the brain systems. A person or a group appears calm and even experiences a level of cognitive peace, but because the robust connection between the limbic system and the cerebral cortex is missing, so is creativity and empathic problem solving.

The second feature of what is known about the brain is the dual hemispheres of the cerebral cortex. Often popularly referred to as "right brain" and "left brain," these two sides of the cerebral cortex have quite different functions.

The right hemisphere generally begins with recognizing the big picture and then moves to consider the individual parts that make up that picture. It is intuitive, spatial, visual, subjective, and quite imaginative. It solves problems by using hunches. It thinks and works spontaneously.

The left hemisphere generally begins with parts or details and then pulls back to recognize a larger picture of the whole. It is rational, linear, sequential, and quite logical. It solves problems by working with as much definitive information as possible, solving problems sequentially and logically. It thinks and works best in a planned and organized way.

Most people have a hemispheric dominance or preference, even though they are physiologically capable of operating simultaneously in a balance of both hemispheres. *Dominance* means "influenced by" and results in a pattern of dealing with life's issues, concerns, and opportunities. This preference is developed through life experience and conditioning. There are few if any circumstances, however, in which a person ever operates completely in one hemisphere. A fuller capacity to respond to the circumstances of life is gained by attention to the balance of the hemispheres.

David Ludwig[44] suggests that there are two kinds of people: painters

---

44 For further information about Ludwig's understanding of types of people, see his *Renewing*

and pointers. Pointers think through things internally; are drawn to bullet points and sequential, linear thinking; and want logical suggestions that lead to logical behavior. They appreciate rules. Painters think through things externally, by means of dreaming dreams and considering larger and broader issues. They want suggestions that point to a greater reality and lead to expansive and entrepreneurial behavior. They tend to press against the boundaries of the ordinary.

Characteristics of the hemispheres are listed in the table below, thanks to Allen Nauss's work.[45]

LEFT HEMISPHERE	RIGHT HEMISPHERE
FAMILIAR	**NOVEL**
VERBAL LANGUAGE	LANGUAGE OF MUSIC, ART, POETRY (VISION-SPATIAL)
1,000 words	picture
words, concepts	metaphors, similes, analogies
analytic	emotional, energetic, bonding, identifying with others
reductionistic, either/or thinking	beauty, ambiguity
conceptual, logical	intuitively perceptive
close lexical/semantic relationships	looser semantic associations
EXPLICIT	IMPLICIT
details, parts, assemblage of parts	generalizations, whole gestalt patterns, context
concrete, linear	abstract, holistic
certainty, definitiveness, inflexibility	undifferentialness, ambiguity, flexibility
focused attention	sustained internal intensity
passivity	activity
sequential	simultaneous
what	how

the *Family Spirit* (St. Louis: Concordia Publishing House, 1989). See also Ludwig's *The Power of We: The Gift of Marriage*: a DVD- and CD-Rom-based Bible study (St. Louis: Concordia Publishing House, 2009).

45 Nauss, *Implications of Brain Research for the Church*, 38.

Andy loved his job as the business manager of his thriving congregation. He took this position believing that better and more efficient office practices would help the church run its business side more effectively and would, therefore, help make life easier for the rest of the staff. The first thing he tackled was creating a schedule for generating the weekly bulletin. He had often heard from Grace, the administrative assistant, that there were problems with timely submissions of bulletin announcements, especially from the music director, Evan, and to a lesser extent, Pastor Michael.

One of the first things Andy did was to establish a deadline of Thursday at noon. That would give him Thursday afternoon to organize the information and get it to Grace on Friday morning so it could be printed on Friday afternoon. Then, Andy would stack the bulletins in the elders' area for distribution for the Saturday evening and Sunday morning worship services.

One of the first things that happened after Andy sent out the schedule was that Evan missed the deadline.

"Andy!" Evan breathlessly yelled as he rushed into the office on Friday morning just before lunch. "I forgot about your deadline, and I need this important announcement in the bulletin."

Andy felt his blood pressure rise, even as he saw out of the corner of his eye that Grace smiled knowingly.

"What was the problem?" Andy asked.

"I forgot about the deadline," Evan said. "But I also didn't have a chance to think through what I needed to say. This is an important announcement, so it was bouncing around for a couple of days. You can get this in the bulletin for me, right?"

"No, I can't," said Andy. "The layout is finished."

"But Grace hasn't printed it yet," countered Evan. "You can do it this once."

Andy took a deep breath, took the announcement, gave it to Grace (who was still smiling), and said, "We'll do it this week, but not after this."

Evan gushed, "You are both terrific! Thanks. You know I have problems paying attention to details and deadlines."

"No, I didn't know that," said Andy, "until now."

Grace now chimed in, "Evan, you point to this as a problem, but in my experience, it's nothing new. After we make the change to this week's bulletin, let's talk about how we can get on the same page."

The meeting took place at 3:00 p.m. on Friday, after the bulletins were finished. Grace began, "I know that being timely has been a challenge for you, Evan, and I think that if it keeps up, Andy will get more and more frustrated. He can just adjust to this, or he can put his foot down. But another possibility is that we talk about what would be helpful for you in this regard. One option is to stop going the way we have in the past. It's best for all of us that we get on the same page."

Evan took some time to describe this aspect of his life and how, even as a student in school, he had difficulty completing assignments on time. As he talked, though, the root cause became apparent to him. "One thing I am beginning to realize is that I have trouble coming to a conclusion about how to say really well what I want to say. I get stuck on many ideas and phrases."

"Would it help you to talk this out with someone?" Grace asked.

"Maybe," Evan admitted.

"Would it work," Andy took up the theme, "for us to meet on Wednesday to talk about what you want to say and, maybe, even how we can help you get done we need you to do?"

"I'll try that," said Evan.

And so they did.

In this hypothetical situation, Andy's hemispheric preference is left, Evan's is right, and Grace's is relatively balanced. Left alone, it would be easy to anticipate an increasing problem between Evan and Andy. But what right-hemisphere-dominant Evan needed was an opportunity to process externally what he was expected to do. Grace had a sense that trouble was coming and that talking would be helpful.

When asked about it later, Grace said, "I really don't know where the idea came from. It just popped into my head."

From right-hemisphere intuition, she had enough confidence to act on it, and she did so with sensitivity to left-hemisphere-dominant Andy, who, when he understood Evan's problem, created a specific next step. In this way, Grace, who is familiar with the brain theory material, was able to help direct her co-workers toward a situation in which resolution was possible.

The situation did not devolve into one of criticism or name calling. Nowhere was there a "you're really a flake and all you want to do is flitter around like a butterfly" from Andy, or "you're a rigid person who just wants to control things" from Evan. There was not a "you are both going to butt heads because of your personality styles, so why don't you fix what's wrong with you" from Grace. There was no need because Grace had an understanding of the differences in hemispheric dominance that may have been contributing to the emerging conflict and offered a healthy next step.

It was late into the meeting of the finance board. The board members were discussing a request from the worship committee for the purchase of a projector and screens for the sanctuary. The new equipment would not interfere with the architecture of the chancel or its surroundings, and members of the congregation who had vision or hearing impairments would sit up front (which they generally did anyway) so they could see the hymns and Scripture readings better and not have to hold the heavy hymnal.

Mack begrudgingly accepted the recommendation, but he was concerned that the worship committee had not conducted a thorough study of the equipment options and that the details of funding the project were not specific enough.

For his part, Leroy was ecstatic about the screens.

As the meeting progressed, the board members on either side became animated and emotions began to run very high. The conversation spiraled as the themes were being repeated.

Mack: "I don't see the step-by-step reality of how we can afford to pay for this equipment. Besides, I don't think we've had an architect plan how the screens would impact the chancel and its surrounding area. Give me more data!"

Leroy: "The Spirit will do His job, and we'll figure it out as we go. If we plan to the last detail, we will never get it done. God will find a way, and we will find God's way, and it will all be okay. Let's get on with it. Put it in the budget. Someone will step up!"

Seeing that the conversation was growing more circular and more heated, Pastor Luke interrupted: "Looks like we're at a bit of a stalemate. Mack thinks we need more concrete data; Leroy wants us to move forward and get it done. I suggest we take a moment or two and rest from the conversation. After a moment or two of contemplation, I will offer a prayer."

After a moment of silence, Pastor Luke prayed: "Dear Jesus, thank You for Your presence with us this evening. You see we are struggling. Leroy and Mack, as well as most all of us, have different needs in order to come to agreement on this question. Guide us to use those differences in ways that help us gather together to do Your work and that help us be together as sisters and brothers in Christ. In Your name we pray, O dear Jesus! Amen."

Leroy: "Thanks, pastor. Let's put off a vote on this. We've got a little time. Mack, can you get the information that you need by next meeting?"

Mack: "I'll make a list of what would be helpful to me. Now that I think about it, a strategy for either raising the money for this or taking it from some other fund in the budget would settle that part of it for me. About the plans—could somebody just make a drawing so I could actually see what it would look like?"

Pastor Luke saw that the meeting was being hijacked by the increasing dominance of the limbic system. Creative thought was diminishing; position taking was happening more and more. By requesting that they take a break, he was hoping that the collective cerebral cortexes would catch up to the rest of the brain systems—and he knew that a reminder of Jesus' presence and call to Jesus in prayer was appropriate and necessary. After the cool-down period and prayer, both Leroy and Mack relaxed their views and agreed to a more cooperative endeavor, at least for a time.

Speaking Personally

Here, I'd like to remind you of three books I've recommended previously: Allen Nauss's *Implications of Brain Research for the Church* and *The Pastor's Brain Manual,* and Holly Inglis's *Sticky Learning*. All have been especially useful to me, and I believe they will be to you, as well, because they take church leaders far beyond the confines of this chapter.

I remember a line that my mother said often: "Count to ten before you say anything bad about anybody." I discovered that when I took a moment to pause, I rarely chose to say anything bad. My mom had no scientific evidence, but as I've shown in this chapter, we know the accuracy of her advice.

I should continue to take it.

Some years ago, I was with the director of the National Institutes of Mental Health. As we were chatting, someone in our group asked him what he thought would be the major mental health challenges of the twenty-first century. First, he said that he thought the mental health challenges of the nineteenth and twentieth centuries were diseases of repression. By this, he meant that a lot of people held emotional experiences inside and that much of mental health efforts had to do with helping people release those emotions. Then he said that he believed the mental health challenges of the twenty-first century would have to do with diseases of impulse control. By this, he meant people not thinking through the implications of their actions but merely acting on their impulses. I think he is right. The description I've used in this chapter is a person who is hijacked by his or her limbic system or R-complex or both.

As electronic communication increased, I began to use emails as a tool for conversation. In the process, I discovered that I was misunderstood more often (at least that is how I defended myself). Even more importantly, I was more often seen as excessively confrontational. As

I reflected on this over time, it became clear my emails were written in the immediate present—more reactive, more write-without-thinking. As I recognized this, I began to write shorter business-oriented emails and all but abandoned potentially controversial email conversations. I suspect that my mom would have said something equivalent to "Should have been listening to me, Bruce." She'd be right. Brain theory supports her as well.

CHAPTER ELEVEN

Different People, Different Ways

People are different. We come in various sizes, shapes, colors, and styles. A chapter of a book is hardly necessary to make that point. It is in the use of those differences that there is room for discussion.

From pre-Christian days to the present time, systems or models have been created to describe people according to different types of personality. For example, the "four humours" is a centuries-old theory of personality types. According to this theory, people were sanguine, choleric, phlegmatic, and melancholy. Each could stand alone as a basic characteristic, or they could be combined into a more nuanced personality style.

These four types had certain characteristics:

Sanguine: amorous, happy, generous, optimistic, irresponsible

Choleric: violent, vengeful, short-tempered, ambitious

Phlegmatic: sluggish, pallid, cowardly

Melancholic: introspective, sentimental, gluttonous[46]

---

46 "The Four Humours," Kheper website, accessed July 27, 2015, www.kheper.net/topics/typology/four_humours.HTML.

Over the years, much more work has been done beyond these ancient four types to develop, identify, and constructively utilize the various natural differences among people.

This echoes the reality described by St. Paul:

> For just as the body is one and has many members, and all the members of the body, though many, are one body, so it is with Christ. For in one Spirit we were all baptized into one body—Jews or Greeks, slaves or free—and all were made to drink of one Spirit.
>
> For the body does not consist of one member but of many. If the foot should say, "Because I am not a hand, I do not belong to the body," that would not make it any less a part of the body. And if the ear should say, "Because I am not an eye, I do not belong to the body," that would not make it any less a part of the body. If the whole body were an eye, where would be the sense of hearing? If the whole body were an ear, where would be the sense of smell? But as it is, God arranged the members in the body, each one of them, as He chose. If all were a single member, where would the body be? As it is, there are many parts, yet one body.
>
> The eye cannot say to the hand, "I have no need of you," nor again the head to the feet, "I have no need of you." . . .
>
> Now you are the body of Christ and individually members of it. (1 Corinthians 12:12–21, 27)

Paul was specifically discussing spiritual gifts and offices—that is, the diversity of functions within the community with all members having concern for one another. Just as God created unique parts of the body to function together, so also does each person in the Body of Christ function together in his or her God-given uniqueness. From here, St. Paul leads into 1 Corinthians 13, which extols the practice of love as the greatest virtue among love, hope, and faith.

This same principle might well be applied to personality types and styles. People perceive things differently and learn differently; they act differently and are motivated by different things; they feel differently and picture the world differently. People are different in fundamental ways. But each person brings something unique to the community table.

What happens when individuals present themselves at the community table depends in many ways on the capacity of church leaders. What would happen to the body if the leader, an eye, demanded that everyone function like him? or if the leader is an ear and only paid attention to other ears? What if the eye only saw other eyes and if the ear only heard other ears? The community would become either one of infinite mirror reflection or an echo chamber.

Here, the first task of church leaders is to recognize their own style; the second task is to share that knowledge and constructively utilize it. There are many ways to investigate style, such as the historic sanguine, choleric, phlegmatic, and melancholic pattern referenced earlier. The Myers-Briggs Type Indicator is widely used for this purpose. "The goal of understanding and using type is to promote the constructive use of differences," says Lynne Baab, paraphrasing Isabel Briggs Myers.[47] Baab herself asserts that personality "type can help church leadership teams work together more effectively. Many church boards study type in order to understand and communicate with each other better."[48]

Another lens through which to look is found at www.insightlearning .com, where they describe a personality spectrum. The objective of the website is as follows:

> This website will help you interact successfully with all types of people by (1) identifying your unique personality style and the styles of those around you, (2) teaching you everything you need to know about all personality types, and (3) showing you how to adjust your behaviors until you consistently treat other people the way they want to be treated.[49]

47 Baab, *Personality Type in Congregations*, xv.
48 Baab, *Personality Type in Congregations*, xiii.
49 Insight Learning, accessed July 27, 2015, www.insightlearning.com/Home.asp.

There are clear assumptions here: "Each of us has something to learn; each something to teach. We are all resources to each other."[50] In this way, differences are valued and utilized. In the process, people are respected and relationship and organizational cohesion grow.

The director of Christian outreach, James, was still a little frustrated but pretty hopeful as well. He had just received his first evaluation that was conducted by the evangelism board, the members of which were Sandy, its chairperson; Curt; Ryan; and Abigail. He liked the comments he read and heard, such as "very friendly and social," "sensitive to other people," "personally well-liked by practically everyone," "gives everyone a voice in meetings," and "draws out others' gifts." These were all ways that he thought he contributed in a positive and useful way. The evangelism board most certainly agreed. But there were the other parts of the evaluation that were more challenging: "needs to be more concerned to get things done on time," "needs to put limits on talking with the other staff members because it interrupts their efficiency," and "sometimes is too enthusiastic."

James recognized that he was often late to finish a task, especially those that required working alone at his desk. He remembered that this was difficult for him all the way through college and that he learned to develop study groups to help him with this. Still, writing papers by himself was a chore. He remembered how he would get restless working in his room and would want to start a conversation with his roommate. This happened enough that his roommate would study at the library to keep from being interrupted. So James would walk the hall, looking for an open door of a friend so that he could go in and talk. It was kind of like that in the office now. People would come in; he would drop everything to talk with them. He never closed his door because he wanted an open environment. "This is really who I am," he remembered saying to the members of the evangelism board. "You hired me for outreach because, among other things, you want me to reach out and to work with others to help them reach out for Christ too."

---

50 Fred Leafgren and Joseph Sullivan, *Personality Effectiveness with Style*, 5.

It was Sandy's response that really helped: "That is why we brought you on board. We admire and affirm your people orientation. You do it well, and we are very positive about you. It seems, though, that you struggle with the challenges of our evaluation of you."

"Hmm . . . ," said James.

Sandy continued: "We affirm you, who you are, and what you bring to the table. It is because we want you to do well and because we care about you that we challenge you. Putting some limits on your connecting with people so that other tasks are done in a timely way is also important—quite important to others who have a different style than you. We'd like to help here. We don't just lay this on you. If you think our challenges are important and are growth areas for you, then let's work on them together."

James mused about what happened: "Sandy challenged me, and that hurt some. But she also connected to me in a warm way. She really seemed to want to help. She actually seemed to have my best interests and our working together at heart. That made it much easier for me to understand what she and the others were saying, and we began to develop some strategies to work on this."

James's style, or type, is interactive and interpersonally oriented. He gains strength and momentum from others. This can be observed about his spiritual life, as he has never been able to develop a consistent private devotional life but loves the consistency of his small group that studies Scripture together weekly. He is sensitive to the needs of others and is empathic toward them. He gains personal strength in doing this and also when others are sensitive to his needs. This is why Sandy's response resonated with him. She encouraged him within the context of caring for him. Sandy recognized James's style, or type, and she was able to meet him on an interpersonal level that was consistent with his style.

However, if other members of the committee had been responding, the tenor of the evaluation might have been quite different. For instance, consider a possible response by Curt:

"This is really who I am," he remembers saying to the members of the evangelism board. "You hired me for outreach because, among

other things, you want me to reach out and to work with others to help them reach out for Christ too."

"Well," said Curt matter-of-factly, "we do need this pattern to change. It takes up too much time for others on the staff, and we need timely performance from you. We want you to log your time during the day and submit those logs to me. The idea is that you close your door when you need to get your work done as well."

It is not that Curt's ideas were bad, nor that he was without care for James. The pattern did need to change; James's work style was affecting the work of others on the staff, and doing a time analysis could actually be helpful. But Curt's style is less personal and more task oriented. He wants things handled directly and challenges met quickly. He likes thought-out plans and evaluations. He is firm and prizes efficiency. Curt's style and James's style clash. Since James's style is interactive and he wants to do well, he would likely acquiesce to Curt's style and demands. But it will be a different kind of conformity than his work with Sandy would be. The Curt-James mix would be one with less enthusiasm and more resistant and passive conformity. The Sandy-James mix would bring cooperative teamwork and a warmer working relationship that would energize James.

Even without formal training in personality styles or types, Sandy was aware of the differences, sought to engage James constructively, and did so quite intuitively. Curt, on the other hand, simply implemented his own work style without effort to understand James. Perhaps Curt was not even aware of his own style. In any case, he did not use an understanding of personality differences.

If another committee member, Ryan, had responded, the outcome might also have been somewhat different.

"This is really who I am," he remembers saying to the members of the evangelism board. "You hired me for outreach because, among other things, you want me to reach out and to work with others to help them reach out for Christ too."

"Hey," Ryan said, gesturing with an open hand, "we have to take this on because it's getting in the way of achieving what we want you

to achieve and what others around you need to be doing as well. Take a risk! Change your ways! Pray for the Holy Spirit! Do it! You're creative, and you care for people. Use it! Make it happen! It will be good for you and for us. And you'll have an even better reputation than you have now. And who knows, you may be called to work for an even larger church one day because of that reputation."

It is not that Ryan was off base or without care for James. Setting necessary or even innovative goals is important. James did need some motivation, and long-term advancement is valid motivation. Ryan's work style is more energetic and entrepreneurial. He likes to make things happen, and often at his own place of employment, he gives pep talks to other salespeople who report to him. He prizes creativity and risk, initiative taking, and challenge acceptance. But his style and James's style clash in this example. Ryan and the evangelism committee are in positions of authority in relationship to James; James recognizes that and will do, albeit reluctantly, what is expected. Ryan wants James to keep his eye on the prize, but James's focus is on people. He will follow through for the sake of the relationship he has with those he serves and with the committee, though probably not for the sake of earning a promotion. The work will continue, but a closer relationship that would energize James is not likely to be achieved.

Like Curt, Ryan implemented his own work style without particular attention to what James actually needed or wanted. Ryan certainly was not self-reflective, and although the immediate outcome would be achieved and there would be some progress as James's work grew timelier and less intrusive on his co-workers' time, the warmth of a close and collegial relationship would be missing.

If Abigail, yet another committee member, had responded, the outcome might have changed significantly.

"This is really who I am," James remembers saying to the members of the evangelism board. "You hired me for outreach because, among other things, you want me to reach out and to work with others to help them reach out for Christ too."

"What do you mean, 'This is really who I am'?" questioned Abigail. "That's an interesting response. I want to know more of what you mean."

James explained the best he could, referencing his college experience and his people-orientation.

"Do you mean that you are unable to change the way that you do things?" Abigail asked calmly.

"Well, no. I guess I can change, maybe," James responded.

"I think you are maybe wondering whether you can do this," she said.

"No, I can change this," James said, somewhat defensively.

"Let's establish a logical plan. I can give you the template for how to plan a change in behavior. And you need to put all this in the context of the larger picture of the vision for your ministry as the director of Christian outreach," said Abigail.

And plan they did. It was a strategic effort, having to do with some of the same things Curt suggested.

It is not that Abigail's ideas were off base, nor was she without care for James. Abigail is logical, persistent, seeks information, and thinks in a linear and systematic way. She is not emotional and is typically formal. She works analytically and relatively impersonally. Abigail is quite competent and enjoys sharing her competency. James will conform to Abigail's demands as well. He is, after all, a people person and will sacrifice some of his own feelings and personal needs and wants for the benefit of pleasing others.

Like Ryan and Curt, Abigail went about dealing with James in a way that was appropriate to her style. Since she is in a position of authority, she could impose her work style or personality type on James and in the current situation. What was critical to James's style—the development of a closer, warmer relationship while the tasks were being accomplished—would not be achieved. He might conform, but he would not draw closer to Abigail.

In all four of these scenarios, James changed his behavior. Therefore, that goal was achieved. But which of the scenarios offered the best opportunity for building up the Body of Christ? Although that opportunity existed in each of these scenarios, the interaction between Sandy and James not only achieved the corporate goal, but it also drew them together into a more personal and vital working relationship, a crucial aspect of James's personality.

The church leader who knows, recognizes, respects, and utilizes the spectrum of styles and personality types has the better potential, blessed by the working of the Holy Spirit, to build up the Body of Christ.

By using any of the style and personality type models, the church leader should be alert to a superficial understanding that devolves into name-calling or labeling. People should be seen as multiple facets of a whole and never be defined by only one trait. One way to keep this in check is to monitor the words used to describe other people, especially in their presence. For example:

Negative	Positive
Too emotional	Warm
Rigid	Stable, sets clear parameters
Heartless	Logical
Flaky	Spontaneous

If church leaders are so inclined, positive words can be found to describe every behavior. Searching for the positive is a way of building up. Additionally, church leaders should resist simply falling back on their work style or personality type to excuse or rationalize their behavior. For instance, an entrepreneurial type, when called to account for advocating a risky venture for the church, should not respond with "Well, that's just the way that I am." Self-reflection and awareness require forthrightness and vulnerability.

Church leaders should also not place style or type preferences into a concrete, never-changing identity for themselves or others. People can and will change. As they seek to build up the community, they will shift, adapt, compromise, learn, and grow. Labeling others should be avoided. Rather, communities of self-reflective people, reflective about themselves and one another, can do their part to mutually build up the

Body of Christ. Indeed, "now you are the body of Christ and individually members of it" (1 Corinthians 12:27).

Speaking Personally

I have found www.insightlearning.com quite helpful over the years. I have used and taught that system in workshop and classroom formats and have been enriched by it. Many churches use aspects of the Myers-Briggs Type Index (MBTI). That is the system Lynne Baab uses in her book *Personality Type in Congregations.* Concordia Seminary in St. Louis has used the MBTI in the past and continues to use the Millon Index of Personality Styles (MIPS) and DiSC, two relatively well-known and often-used tests of personality and leadership characteristics. These help future pastors and deaconesses reflect on aspects of who they are as people and what their personality characteristics are. These characteristics will, of course, directly influence their behavior, and their behavior will directly influence their ministry.

When I first came to Concordia Seminary as a professor, the first class I taught was an elective. At first, I taught it consistently with aspects of my own personality style: we covered five areas vital to understanding human experience, and we got to them as the class dynamic and process allowed. The syllabus was brief and did not identify meeting topics to be covered in class sessions. In other words, it was a very nonlinear and quite loose syllabus. Before long, there was a general restlessness among the students. Their general complaint: we want more organization. Were they just rebellious students? No. Rather, they had difficulty connecting with my personality style, which drove my approach to teaching that class. In response, I devised a new syllabus that was linear and defined what we were doing in each class. Those students were able to give voice to their need that came from their style. Thankfully, I could respond without getting too defensive.

I highly regard church leaders who seek to surround themselves with people who are different than they are, who can bring differing perspectives and personal styles to the table. This does not mean, of course, that anything goes. But it does mean that ears, eyes, noses, feet, hands, and so forth do make up the body.

CHAPTER TWELVE

Conflict Intensity

Conflict is often seen as a bad thing, something to be avoided as much as possible. For many, conflict is a sign of problems. However, conflict is necessary and, because people have differences, it is a normal aspect of human existence. It is necessary for creative solutions to challenges and for personal growth. It is when conflict is suppressed or becomes destructive that there are problems. If there is too little conflict, then there is an organizational or personal stagnation. When there is too much conflict, especially conflict that escalates and becomes personal, then there is increasing damage and the distance between people expands. Church leadership includes managing conflict in such a way that it is useful and helpful, stimulating and energizing.

Management of the conflict is crucial. One of the early tasks in dealing with conflict is to identify its intensity level. This is especially important in a church-related conflict where the deeper levels of conflict may not be as easily recognized. For instance, church leaders believe they are working together on a project, cooperating with others on the committee by exchanging ideas and perspectives in order to reach a creative solution, when an underlying conflict derails the project. Perhaps the conflict is competition as to who will win this battle, or even a hostile,"I'll be pleasant, but I am really out to get you."

Sam Leonard offers an outline of conflict intensity in his book *Mediation: The Book: A Step-by-Step Guide for Dispute Resolvers.*[51] For our purposes in *Building Up the Body of Christ,* his outline is adapted below.

CONFLICT INTENSITY . . .

LACK OF CONFLICT

Here, there is little, if any, growth. Change is excessively slow. Organizations at this level tend to be where the proverbial "circle the wagons" is in place. There is no opportunity for internal dispute, challenging accepted practices, or expressing alternative viewpoints. Creativity does not blossom because differing ideas, opinions, and strategies do not have a place to be shared. Conflict, if it exists, remains locked inside the individuals who wish to remain a part of the relationship or the organization.

Julia was the newest member of the board for Christian education, and this was her first meeting. The principal, Elizabeth, began the meeting with prayer. Then Samuel, the elected chairperson of the board, conducted the meeting.

The meeting consisted of Elizabeth's recommendations for changing several school policies; Samuel supported each of the recommendations. In each case, there was little discussion and votes were unanimous.

Julia also voted for all the recommendations, although she was aware she was not fully informed about them. She went home satisfied with the meeting, commenting to her husband about its efficiency and peacefulness. She looked forward to serving on this board. In her experience at her previous church, board meetings were characterized by a lot of fighting, so this seemed so wonderful to her.

---

51 Leonard, *Mediation*, 38–42.

Low-Grade Conflict

Here, something just does not feel right, but there is not yet enough information to identify what it is. At this level, organizations and the people within them tend to be a bit uneasy. There continue to be practically no opportunities for differing opinions or the expression of feelings that something is uncomfortable. A few mumblings about this discomfort might be heard. Generally, the focus (if there is one) is on consistency, so creativity continues to stagnate. Conflict may be sensed but not identified. However, there may be movement as the low-grade conflict festers, although it still may not have a clear voice.

Julia was the newest member of the board for Christian education, and this was her first meeting. The principal, Elizabeth, began the meeting with prayer. Then Samuel, the elected chairperson of the board, conducted the meeting.

The meeting consisted of Elizabeth's recommendations for changing several school policies; Samuel supported each of the recommendations. In each case, there was little discussion and votes were unanimous.

Julia also voted for all the recommendations, although she was aware she was not fully informed about them. She went home a bit perplexed and uncomfortable. Things went well at the meeting, but there was little discussion and a total absence of questioning, much less active disagreement. Something did not sit well with her. She looked forward to serving on this board and was glad that there was no active and interminable conflict, as there had been in her previous experience. But still . . . where were the questions, the challenges, or even the disagreements? Julia resolved to ask about this characteristic if the same pattern was evident in the next meeting.

Problem-to-Be-Solved

Here, the concern, problem, or opportunity is known, identified, spoken about, and worked on. In acknowledging the issue, an organization and the people within it focus on clearly defining the situation; gathering information, ideas, and opinions; and mobilizing resources to address it. A major organizational characteristic here is robust collaboration in which people come together to express their thoughts, ideas, and strategies. The major emotional energy is to solve the problem, engage the opportunity, and move forward to master the challenge. The focus is clearly on what needs to be faced. Characteristic of this stage is "we are working together to solve the problem or to engage the challenge," using a strategy of bringing people of varying perspectives together in order to solve the problem. Conflict is seen as different perspectives on the problem to be solved.

Julia was the newest member of the board for Christian education, and this was her first meeting. The principal, Elizabeth, began the meeting with prayer. Then, Samuel, the elected chairperson of the board, conducted the meeting. The meeting consisted of Elizabeth's recommendations for changing several school policies.

Three days before the meeting, every committee member, including Elizabeth, had received a complete written brief detailing the rationale for the changes. Samuel began the discussion by first asking for questions about the content of the recommendations and the rationale. After that discussion, he asked for opinions and concerns committee members had about the changes. Every committee member was invited to speak. The questions were generally informed and crisp and often generated comments and other questions. Everyone was involved in the decision. Then, a formal vote was taken, even though the conversation brought forward a consensus.

Julia was thrilled and excited about serving on this board. Conversation was rich and plentiful; everyone was informed; all participated; and differences were respectfully aired, heard, and discussed. The energy of this board was really electric.

Personal Debate

Here, persuasion begins to be the goal of conversation, over solving the problem or engaging the challenge. Certainly, the challenge remains, but the conversations turn sharper and the goal appears to be

144

winning the debate. The emotional energy has changed and the issues have become personal. The intensity of the conflict can quickly ramp up. One of the chief problems of this level of intensity is that personhood gets mixed up with the problem to be solved. It is no longer "We are working together to solve the problem or to engage the challenge." Rather, it is "You have a different idea than I have and because you have a different idea, something is wrong with you." Personal attacks can take place at this stage. Since very few people like to be attacked, those who are attacked will want to defend themselves. Again, the conversation is focused on personal characteristics more than on the problem to be solved. The goal is to persuade or to force conformity, insinuating that a differing view is a fault in the other person.

Julia was the newest member of the board for Christian education, and this was her first meeting. The principal, Elizabeth, began the meeting with prayer. Then, Samuel, the elected chairperson of the board, conducted the meeting. The meeting consisted of Elizabeth's recommendations for changing several school policies.

Three days before the meeting, every committee member, including Elizabeth, had received a complete written brief detailing the rationale for the changes. Samuel began the discussion by first asking for questions about the content of the recommendations and the rationale. After that discussion, he asked for opinions and concerns committee members had about the changes.

Every committee member was invited to speak. In a flash, one committee member criticized Elizabeth about the recommendations, suggesting that she was attempting to usurp too much authority. Another criticized Samuel for not showing enough leadership and letting Elizabeth "run the show." A third member criticized one of the other members of not being "Christian" in his tone and responses.

Tempers flared; voices raised. The recommendations were passed, but several people left angry and uncomfortable.

"Wow," Julia said to herself as she left. "What have I gotten myself into?"

WIN/LOSE COMPETITION

Here, the battle lines are drawn, sides are identified, groups are formed, and strategies are developed: the goal is to win. By this time in the growth of the intensity of a conflict, emotional energy has been significantly diverted from problem-solving to winning the contest. The conflict is as much or more about power to win than it is about solving the problem or engaging the challenge. Organizations at this level have factions and groups with, often, clearly identified positions that mobilize people to take on the battle and to win it. Whether a particular position is the most creative and useful way to problem solve is not open to question, because the emotional goal is winning. In every battle like this, there is a winner and, obviously, a loser. Most often, people do not like to lose. So if behaviors are stuck here, then much emotional energy is consumed in ongoing battle. Creativity to address the problem or engage the challenge is greatly lessened. But it can get even worse.

Julia was the newest member of the board for Christian education, and this was her first meeting. . . .

Tempers flared; voices raised. During the animated discussion, both Elizabeth and Samuel were counting potential votes. There were six board members present. Two were opposing the recommendations and criticizing Samuel and Elizabeth. Three had spoken in support of Elizabeth and Samuel. Julia had been quiet and had not participated in the discussion.

Samuel was confident that there were enough votes to pass the recommendations, so he motioned to one of the supporting board members to "call the question," which passed three to two. Julia abstained from voting, saying she was not sufficiently apprised of the issues to responsibly vote. After that, each recommendation passed three to two.

After the meeting, members of both groups attempted to corner Julia to enlist her alignment with their group.

FIGHT/FLIGHT

Here, there is more and more hostility and, eventually, a division in the relationship (either actually or emotionally). The other side is now the opposition or even the enemy.

In such a fight, people do get hurt. Yet that outcome is not important in this situation because the conflict itself—and winning it—is more important than harm to people or problem-solving. When conflict has reached this intensity, people may believe that the problem is other people, and if those other people can simply be defeated, then everything will be all right. People who lose the battle leave, perhaps to battle in a different way at another time. Regardless, energy is put into the battle. Whatever the original problem or challenge was is now part of an irrelevant past. All that remains is the fight.

The group of two indicated to Julia that they were going to resign from the board in protest to the "arrogant and authoritarian leadership" of Elizabeth and Samuel. They said they would publicly resign at the voters assembly the following month. They would also call other members of the congregation to join them in protest.

After the two left, the group of three approached Julia with their own reaction to the meeting, indicating that they thought the two were troublemakers and "not good for much except fighting."

As Julia started on her way home, she wondered what she had gotten herself into and if she should even stay on the board.

SEARCH AND DESTROY

Here, there is a total breakdown in connection and communication. People on the other side of the issue are no longer seen as individuals, as people in their own right; instead, they are seen as part of the enemy. People are part of a group that should be opposed and not only defeated, but also destroyed. Empathy for the person is no longer practiced. War results.

The group of two indicated that they would be calling for the removal of Elizabeth as principal and Samuel as board chair because of their "failure of leadership" and their "arrogant and authoritarian personalities."

The group of three indicated that they would seek the removal of the two from the board because they were "chronic attackers" and "brought no good things to the table."

"The way they all act, they must be having difficulties at work or home," Julia thought. She was beginning to wonder, in addition to everything else, if she had joined the right congregation.

ANNIHILATION

Wipe them all out! Destroy all the opposition! (Enough said.)

One can only speculate, sadly, what the next days will bring as both sides prepare for battle at the voters assembly.

As the conflict intensity increases beyond the problem-to-be-solved level, individuals are seen less and less as people and more as a conglomerate. It is necessary to take personhood away from people in order to justify attack, destruction, and annihilation. The very thing that characterizes the Body of Christ—respect for all components of it—is abandoned.

The sweet spot in conflict management is the third level: problem to be solved. Here, all the energy that likely was suppressed in the lack of conflict and low-grade conflict levels can be mobilized to solve the problem, engage the challenge, or work on the opportunity. Here, all the energy that was directed toward personalizing the conflict in higher levels (so it moves toward aggression and attack) is reclaimed by working together toward resolution. Church leaders need to recognize the level of conflict they are in and develop ways to facilitate conflict management so that it moves toward the problem to be solved.

One of the first tasks for a leader in the actual conflict management is to determine the level of intensity of the conflict. Different levels of intensity demand different responses. In all situations, however, the leadership goal is to move toward solving the problem.

George Bullard has also developed a seven-point conflict intensity scale.[52] The first three levels of conflict are needed for a congregation to thrive and be built up, but the third level is fraught with some serious danger. Levels four through seven have little potential to build up the Body of Christ. Here is a list of Bullard's levels:

1. Typical Issues with Many Solutions

2. Common Disagreements over Multiple Issues

3. Competition That Develops Causes

4. Now It's Time to Vote or Else

5. Dividing the Medes from the Persians

6. Discrediting Our Enemies

7. Destroying the Infidels

Intensity scales like Bullard's and Leonard's point to the reality that not all conflict is at the same level; that some conflict is natural, necessary, and productive; and that it is imperative that church leaders identify the level of conflict in which they are operating. There is a general sense in the literature that there is healthy and unhealthy conflict, although Stephen Ministries has used the words *robust conversation* to distinguish healthy processes of disagreement from unhealthy ones, which they label *conflict*.

It is also imperative for church leaders to see, in the midst of conflict, where the intensity is most likely to increase. The clearest point at which conflicts begin to increase in intensity is when person and problem become intermixed. People begin to expend energy against one another and away from solving the conflict. The conversation no longer is "we are working on an opportunity together" but rather "there must be something wrong with you that you have that opinion." Church leaders should prevent this movement into a higher level of intensity because it does not build up the Body of Christ. It does nothing but tear it down by attacking the people in it.

---

52 Bullard, *Every Congregation Needs a Little Conflict*, 17.

In almost every conflict except those at higher levels of intensity, the church leader employs a multitude of skills including listening, understanding, and empathy. Showing understanding often soothes even the most irate person to the point that conflict lessens. Facilitating putting boundaries around hurtful behaviors done in the midst of a conflict begins to create a safe space. Allowing space for all voices to be heard and to protect those voices so they continue to be heard fosters more participation and, eventually, more ownership.

Human beings share with almost all the other creatures the capacity to deal with conflict. They can submit or fight or freeze or flee.

To fight, humans may insist, blame, criticize.

To submit, humans may give in or give up, or just agree to be done with it.

To flee, humans may withdraw from a conversation or even leave the area.

To freeze, humans may simply do nothing.[53]

Again, in all these situations, humans share responses with most of the rest of the creatures on this earth. Only humans, however, can talk and listen, become informed, think things over, and dialogue with others. They can pray, hear and meditate on God's Word, and give thanks for the community that God in Christ gives.

Speaking Personally

I wonder if the comment by the director of the National Institute of Mental Health, whom I mentioned earlier, might shed some light on what I see as an increasing problem: conflict is escalating beyond the "problem-to-be-solved" level. Slogans, labels, and attacks run apace, and, sometimes, amok. Social media posts often contain inciting and provocative personal attacks, acting as echo chambers for reinforcing limbic and R-complex–driven behavior.

---

53 Heitler, *From Conflict to Resolution*, 59.

During a conversation with someone who works in politics, I asked about campaign strategies for an upcoming state election. The person said something like "We spend the time before Labor Day attacking the person of our opponent. If that strategy is successful, then the real issues will not be heard. The voter has already turned away from the other candidate." It seemed to me that just about every candidate used the same strategy, although the attack ads did not cease the day after Labor Day. I longed for conversations about substantive issues, but I recognized that to a certain extent, I had succumbed because I was thinking of a candidate I disagreed with as having a bad character. That brought me to repentance quite quickly. (But how easy it was to be moved in that direction!)

I flee to the cross, beg Christ's forgiveness, and beseech the Holy Spirit to equip me with a more discerning eye. And I surround myself with people who will challenge me if I succumb again.

There are many books besides this one about this chapter's topic that I recommend. Among them are George Bullard's *Every Congregation Needs a Little Conflict* and Sam Leonard's *Mediation: The Book: A Step-by-Step Guide for Dispute Resolvers*, both of which I mentioned earlier in this chapter. If you want to delve more deeply into this field, then pick up Susan Heitler's *From Conflict to Resolution*.

CHAPTER THIRTEEN

Conflict Management

The next task in conflict management, after assessing the intensity of the conflict, is to apply skills that are appropriate to the task, beginning with listening and reflecting, as previously discussed. (See page 150.)

Often in conflict, both parties need, want, and even demand airtime. Their verbal and nonverbal energy may be directed toward either blaming the other party or defending themselves. When this occurs, the conflict to be resolved is neglected or even abandoned. This is true at the personal debate, win/lose competition, fight/flight, search and destroy, and annihilation levels.

Listening skills are especially useful to church leaders, whether they are involved in conflicts or simply facilitators in conflict-resolution situations, and allow leaders to work toward reducing the level of intensity. (This is, of course, much more difficult in the more intense conflict stages of search and destroy or annihilation.) The basic move is to seek to understand the opposing viewpoint. Listening and then reflecting on what was heard can help uncover the content of the conflict, which is not necessarily driving the behavior.

"Whose need to talk is greater?"

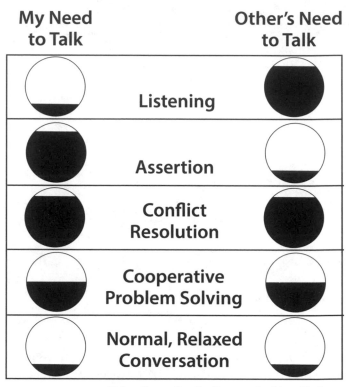

Ridge Consultants, Cazenovia, New York

Susan Heitler's classic book *From Conflict to Resolution* was one of the early resources to point this out. Conflict resolution requires diving underneath that which is seen to explore underlying concerns:

> Positions are initial statements of what one wants. A conflict generally begins when two or more wishes are perceived to oppose one another. . . . The negotiation literature uses the term "positions" to denote opening wishes and from this term derives the phrase "positional bargaining." . . . Initial positions may suggest incompatible plans of action when

in fact the participants' underlying concerns are quite consonant. In these cases, needless conflicts can result. . . .

A concern, on the other hand, is a thought stemming from a value, feeling, desire, preference, fear, or other factor. Concerns usually have "I" as the subject. Because they are subjective and descriptive, not objective or prescriptive, concerns need to be heard nonjudgmentally and accepted at face value. Concerns define the parameters of a problem and therefore serve, consciously or unconsciously, as the criteria for successful resolution.[54]

There may be more agreement between persons in conflict, therefore, if an exploration of the underlying concerns reveals similarity, with the differences occurring at Heitler's position level, the area of the presenting position rather than the underlying concern. If so, then both parties arrive at a problem-solving place, where they put their energy into concrete ways to deal with the underlying concerns.

Using this model, it is critical that church leaders do not take up a position of conflict without an exploration of the underlying concern. If the position is challenged, then conflict will revolve around the position

---

54 Heitler, *From Conflict to Resolution*, 23.

and not the concerns. The question thus becomes, how do church leaders facilitate the identification and exploration of underlying concerns?

The simple answer is to use listening skills, and to use them in the following manner:

1. In the midst of a conflict, both parties have a great desire to talk. Yield the floor. Give enough space for each person to communicate. The leader should be responsive, but be quiet and . . .

2. Use listening and reflecting skills. Keep responses going, continuing to listen and to reflect content and emotions, until there is better understanding of the nature of the conflict. Do not move away from this pattern until there is a full picture and the people involved in the conflict indicate that they understand and are understood. This occurs not just in assertions that understanding is achieved; understanding must be demonstrated.

This approach is useful both when the church leader is directly involved in the conflict and also when he or she is mediating a conflict between others. The first task is to listen and understand.

But that simple step is not always so easy to take. It requires much of the personal capacity discussed earlier in this book, such as trustworthiness, responsiveness to others, transparency and openness, and recognition of personality differences. Nevertheless, church leaders are called to grow in the Spirit and are empowered by this same Spirit.

Nancy had been a member of St. Luke's Church from the time of her birth until the age of twenty-three, when she moved away with her new husband. Now, forty-five years later, she was returning to St. Luke's. This was her childhood church, but she had not been back to the town and the church since her parents had moved from the area.

Over the years, the inside of the church had been totally renovated. Louis, the head elder, knew Nancy was coming because she had called the week before and he had agreed to meet with her after the service to give her a tour of the renovated church.

The conversation began with an introduction and a sharing of the history that Nancy had with the congregation.

"What do you think of the changes we've made since you were last here?" Louis asked.

"I really don't like this more modern stuff," Nancy said. "I like traditional things, and this altar out from the wall and people walking around it and newfangled things like that . . . well, I really don't like it. I suppose it's good for you, but I like the old style better."

Louis was an active participant in planning the renovation, so Nancy's comments stirred up some defensiveness inside him. But he also knew that he wanted to be sure he more fully understood Nancy's position. "The changes that you see are not happy ones for you. You remember and like the old way it was, and this new change is at least a bit . . . well . . . distressing to you."

"You bet it is," Nancy continued. "Not that I really have any say in it. It's just that there were some things in the old church that I thought were really neat and I can't imagine why you would move in such a modern direction when the old things were so meaningful."

"We changed things in the renovation, and that change has taken away some things that were important to you," Louis responded.

"Right," said Nancy. "Why, that old wooden cross that used to be above the altar on the wall . . . that was very nice. It helped me remember what Christ did for us, and now that metal cross hanging from the ceiling looks too modern. And it is hard to see."

"It's hard to not see things that were meaningful to you long ago," Louis said. "Let's take a little walk," he suggested.

Part of the renovation included the construction of a small prayer chapel that was not immediately visible from the renovated sanctuary. When Nancy walked through the doors into the chapel, she stopped and froze. There was the old altar and, on the wall, the wooden cross that she remembered from her childhood.

"We wanted to save these for continuing use, but also as a reminder of the importance of our history. Many, many people like you have looked on this cross and been reminded of the work of Christ."

Startled, Nancy said, "I am sure many people like me have. Did you know that my parents gave the money for that cross in honor of my grandparents?"

"No, I didn't know that," answered Louis. *"But I am glad I know that now."*

"I am glad you saved the cross and that it continues to have meaning for people," observed Nancy.

"I am glad too," Louis said.

The tour continued, and on the way out, Nancy said, "Louis, thanks for showing me around. Actually, I think the renovated church looks okay."

The characteristics of this conversation included careful listening on Louis's part, reflecting what he heard, and openness to further discussion. He was aware of his immediate defensive response, but he corralled that and focused on listening. The result was that the conversation continued and he got to the concern: something in the old church was very important to Nancy. The conversation did not become a debate about the architectural direction. Rather, the conversation became personal and meaningful.

How different the conversation might have been if the following had occurred:

"What do you think of the changes we've made to the inside of the church since you were last here?" Louis asked.

"I really don't like this more modern stuff," Nancy answered. *"I like traditional things, and this altar out from the wall and people walking around it and newfangled things like that . . . well, I really don't like it. I suppose it's good for you, but I like the old style better."*

Louis said, "Modern styles like this are our way of attracting younger people. We want to be a congregation that reaches out into the community."

"You think that a building like this will actually help you reach out in the community?" Nancy asked.

"Our research suggests that it will."

"Show me the research and your attendance numbers since you renovated," she challenged.

In this version of the conversation, Louis responds to Nancy's position statement. He was feeling defensive and asserted his own position statement, neither reflecting the content of Nancy's remark nor the emotions connected with it. Nancy takes up the challenge. After all, she is, in a subtle way, being attacked for not liking something that is outreach oriented. If the conversation were taken further, it might attack her person because she was not being outreach-oriented. This version of the conversation is stuck at the debate level and could deteriorate further.

Next, consider this version of the conversation:

"What do you think of the changes we've made to the inside of the church since you were last here?" Louis asked.

"I really don't like this more modern stuff," Nancy answered. "I like traditional things, and this altar out from the wall and people walking around it and newfangled things like that . . . well, I really don't like it. I suppose it's good for you, but I like the old style better."

"How long has it been since you have been inside of St. Luke's?"

"Maybe forty years," Nancy said.

"Long time."

"Yes," Nancy agreed. "A lot of time has passed. How many pastors have you had over that time?"

Nancy and Louis walked as Louis catalogued the pastoral history. When they reached the narthex, Louis said, "It was nice meeting you, Nancy. Would you like to sign our guest book?"

"Nice to meet you too," Nancy said. She signed the guest book and left.

In this version, the tour was abbreviated, and Nancy didn't see the chapel. Louis essentially ignored Nancy's position and, by changing the subject, communicated that he was not interested in her opinion. There could be a number of reasons why Louis took that step, but his motivation is not as important as his behavior. By ignoring Nancy's position and, especially, by not listening carefully and reflecting, he shut down the conversation. Nancy did her part as well.

The conflict management task here is to go deeper into the conversation to see if concerns can be identified and addressed. The effective church leader makes it a priority to look for, identify, and positively engage the underlying concerns of people in conflict.

Two more examples:

Position: *I don't like the way the flowers are arranged on the altar!*

Possible concerns:

I want the church to look nice for visitors.

I want to be proud of how the church looks.

I am a florist and you should be buying these arrangements from me. I would do a better job.

Position: *We will change hymnals over my dead body!*

Possible concerns:

My mother taught me that the hymnal we have now is all we should ever use, and I would be disloyal to her memory if I supported doing anything differently.

I might lose my way at first and be embarrassed.

My boss tells me to do things I don't like, and I'm not going to be pushed around here too.

There is always a concern underlying a position. Listening helps a church leader uncover it and pay attention to it.

Following the assessment of the intensity of the conflict and gaining a deeper understanding of the concerns of those involved in the conflict, the church leader may still be in a position of conflict. The conflict was resolved in Louis and Nancy's case, but some conflicts are still active even after the concerns are revealed.

The next step is to ask, "What do you hope discussing this with me will achieve?" or "What do you want me to do now that I know your concern?" This kind of question helps to define what the person or persons in the conflict want. For example, perhaps what the person wants and needs is simply to be heard and understood. That is a basic human need, and at times, it is enough to manage the conflict. Sometimes, though, there is more to do.

For instance, in the first example above, one of the hopes for the conversation might be "Give me the flower contract." In the second, the hope might be "Stop the process and keep the hymnals we have." Asking what the person wants in order to resolve the conflict gives the church leader an opportunity to respond with what he or she is willing to do. It also offers an opportunity to see if the other person is now open to hearing the position and concerns of the leader. This part of the conversation might flow this way:

Outcome wanted: *Give me the flower contract.*

Leader response: *I hear from you clearly that you would like the contract. However, I am not in a position to offer that to you. We are happy with our current provider, but if you would like to bid when the contract is up, I can tell you whom to talk to and even give her a heads-up that you will be calling her.*

Outcome wanted: *Stop the process and keep the hymnals we have.*

Leader response: *Clearly, this is a powerful issue that has lots of emotions connected with it. However, I will not and, actually, cannot stop the process. We are getting the new hymnals. I am willing to help you adapt to this change, and I want to walk with you through it, but we are changing hymnals. I'd like to tell you some of our reasoning for that if you are open to hearing it.*

There are times when it is not possible to deal with a conflict by finding a common concern or by changing a concern of one's own. In that case, the ongoing disagreement is acknowledged, but the intention of continuing the relationship and the invitation to do so are clear. Here, there is not a reason to break off relationships when there is a disagreement. Part of the reality of being different people in the Body of Christ is that people have different ideas, positions, and concerns. Using St. Paul's picture in 1 Corinthians 12, the nose's principal concern is to breathe and the ear's is to hear. While the common concern is continuing to give life to the body, their individual tasks are quite different. And although different, they stay in relationship to the body.

There are many models of conflict management, and most of them have these steps in common:

- Assess the intensity of the conflict
- Give airtime to the other person
- Use that airtime to listen and reflect, with the goal of understanding the deeper issues that drive the present conflict
- Determine what is possible to do
- Offer the opportunity for the speaking of one's own positions and concerns
- keep the relationship active by staying in touch with the person

Dr. Dike Drummond offers one such model. He calls it a Universal Upset Patient Protocol (UUPP). This communication protocol is a simple model that offers the opportunity for a leader to help manage conflict, and it is quite congruent with this discussion:

1. Feelings first. For whatever reason, the person is upset. Recognize the feeling.

2. Content next. Encourage the upset person to tell you the nature of his or her trouble.

3. Empathize with the person's situation. This does not mean you agree; rather it means you connect with the discomfort.

4. Ask what the person wants you to do. There may be a specific request here.

5. Say what you are willing to do or what you think should be done.

6. Thanks! Affirm the relationship as one where the person is willing to share what is upsetting to him or her.[55]

Responses like defending oneself, attempting to fix the conflict prematurely before fully understanding it, changing the subject (which

---

55 Dike Drummond, "Doctor Patient Communication—The Universal Upset Patient Protocol," *The Happy MD Blog*, accessed July 27, 2015, www.thehappymd.com/blog/bid/290399/Doctor-Patient-Communication-The-Universal-Upset-Patient-Protocol.

serves to ignore the conflict), or criticizing the person for his or her communication are likely either to inflame the conflict or to break the relationship. Such responses are poor ways to manage conflict, and none of these outcomes are what church leaders want. This is why creative and engaging skills of church leaders, blessed by the Holy Spirit, are so vital.

There is one reminder that bears repeating in conflict management: when a conversation begins to heat up, church leaders must return to listening, reflecting, and searching for the deeper meanings. These are not easy tasks, but they are necessary. Listening is our first duty to our sisters and brothers in Christ.

Speaking Personally

Remember the story of Louis and Nancy? It was based on my own experience with my aunt when we visited the church where we both had grown up. The old church had been torn down and a new one built. My aunt was antagonistic about the new building until she went to the side chapel and saw the cross there, a gift from her and her siblings (including my mother) in honor of their parents (my grandparents).

I did not have much understanding of what was going on at the time, but I clearly remember the incident as an example of the principles described here: what is first presented as a problem may be only the superficial or lightning-rod issue. Listen carefully and you may find some underlying concerns.

I did not dispute with my aunt about architecture, although I liked the contemporary design of the building; I simply gave her space to talk. I am grateful that in the sacred space of the sanctuary, the Holy Spirit helped me be quiet and actively engaged in finding out what was really bothering her.

It is difficult to communicate on the written page how much I think this way of managing conflict is important and how underutilized it is in our churches. I also admit that it is hard to do, or at least it is hard for me. When I feel strongly about something, I so very much want to make my case; that is my emotional interest. I confess that I have to work to corral that and to remind myself that I often do not well understand the position and the concern of the other person. When I remember that, I return to listening. When I better understand the position of the other person, and when he or she acknowledges that I do, then I hope the other person hears me as well. From understanding, we often find common ground, a joint interest on which to work together. We have not necessarily agreed. Rather, we have joined together because we have found an underlying issue that is of concern to us both.

For further reading, I have found Jeffrey Kottler's *Beyond Blame: A New Way of Resolving Conflicts in Relationships* quite helpful. John Hirsch, an LCMS pastor and retired director of congregational and worker care for the Texas District of the LCMS, has penned *The Process of Reconciliation.* This is a very good read for personal, small group, and Bible study work. Consider also reviewing chapter 6 of this book.

CHAPTER FOURTEEN

Conflict Encouragement

"Precisely because they have misled My people, saying, 'Peace,' when there is no peace, and because, when the people build a wall, these prophets smear it with whitewash, say to those who smear it with whitewash that it shall fall!" (Ezekiel 13:10–11a)

"They have healed the wound of My people lightly, saying, 'Peace, peace,' when there is no peace." (Jeremiah 6:14)

The contexts of Ezekiel and Jeremiah are likely different from those of most Christian congregations. But both prophets point to a significant reality in their midst and sometimes in the midst of church leaders as well. The claim is that everyone agrees, when that is not actually so. The proclamation is that there is peace; the reality is that there is conflict. The conflict is either hidden inside a person, is simply not discussed, or goes underground and is discussed in secret.

At milder levels of this dynamic, a church committee member who disagrees with the direction the committee chair wants to go (and the chair has the support of most everyone else) will keep silent during the meeting. Relationships with all the committee members are warm; it is refreshing to spend time together at the committee meeting because everyone has a pretty good time and gets along. This committee member is not willing to rock the proverbial boat, as it might disrupt the goodwill the members believe they have with one another. Personal silence, then, becomes the basic strategy.

The disadvantages of this strategy are at least twofold: (1) the committee does not get the perspective of the member nor the creative input he or she might bring, and (2) suppressed concerns and emotions might find expression among other church members in the church parking lot, in a different context, or at home.

This dynamic requires people to have the same opinion, at least publicly, in order to be together comfortably. In other words, "We will be friends as long as we agree," or "We expect everyone to agree with the committee chair." Silence or verbal agreement during the meeting become the strategy regardless of what a person is actually thinking. Systems-oriented theorists like Ronald Richardson call this kind of group dynamic "enmeshed." "Walter Lippman once said, 'When all think alike, no one thinks very much.' There is a low level of tolerance for differences in thinking, feeling and doing."[56]

In this context, church leaders need to encourage conflict. In Bullard's words: "Every congregation needs a little conflict. Why? Because congregations without conflict are dead or dying. Conflict is a typical, common component of life. A byproduct of conflict is energy and passion. Conflict forces decisions and actions."[57]

In order to think this way, the word *conflict* needs to be redeemed or other words need to be used instead. Synonyms such as "difference of opinion," "another idea," or "alternative thoughts" might serve well. Stephen Ministries has sometimes substituted the phrase "robust conversation" for the healthy characteristics of conflict and reserved the word *conflict* for the darker and more intense interactions associated with competition, strife, or dissent.

Whatever word or words are chosen, St. Paul's notion of both unity in the Body of Christ amongst different people with different gifts

56 Richardson, *Creating a Healthier Church*, 105.
57 Bullard, *Every Congregation Needs a Little Conflict*, 8.

(see Ephesians 4) and the reality that there is a distribution of gifts (see 1 Corinthians 12) helps build a model that utilizes, incorporates, and engages differences. Here, church leaders see to it that differences emerge to be used in healthy conflict in the Body of Christ, all oriented toward the Body's growth and the development of acts of service and ministry.

This form of healthy conflict is necessary for growth and for the creative meeting of challenges and opportunities. It is valued and encouraged. Power and control are not the dominant motivators, but rather collegial conversation and consensus building are dominant. "Problem to be solved" is the sweet spot of work together. Personalities do not become the issue in the conflict. People speak face-to-face. Differences are acknowledged and even encouraged. People make sure they understand the positions of others before they share their own ideas. Respect for the other as redeemed by Christ is normative. The blessing of the Holy Spirit is implored. Helping each person share his or her ideas, thoughts, and feelings becomes a central church leadership task.

We heard about Jane in chapter 7. Here she is again:

Jane was the newly appointed chair of the religious education committee at her congregation. She had served as a member for the last two years. This was her first meeting as the chair. The first item on the agenda was a discussion of the declining Sunday school enrollment. The decline had been moderate over the last several years, but it was consistent and now quite noticeable. Previous attempts to strategize about this were met with suggestions from the part-time director of Christian education, Ellery, and were generally accepted by the committee. The sequence was that a concern would be raised at a regular committee meeting one month; the next month, Ellery would come with a suggestion or recommendation; the committee would vote; and the meeting would be adjourned. There was little discussion and no dissenting views. Jane wondered about the lack of energy within the committee itself and specifically about the absence of discussion, questioning, additional suggestions, and robust conversation. "There is no obvious conflict here," thought Jane, "but the energy I would expect to be part of the meeting is missing. Something is up, but I can't put my finger on it."

Jane created an agenda for the meeting, which had only one item of business: full-range discussion of the Sunday school, its current opportunities and challenges, and its future. The agenda was bracketed by an opening devotion and prayer and closing prayer led by one of the members of the committee. The agenda was distributed a week in advance:

AGENDA
RELIGIOUS EDUCATION COMMITTEE
June XX, XXXX

7:00–8:30 p.m.

1. Gathering (The room will be open by 6:45 p.m.;
   the meeting will begin promptly at 7:00 p.m.)

2. Devotion and prayer (Frank)

3. Open discussion: challenge and opportunities for the
   Sunday school (everyone)

4. Next steps we agree to take (everyone)

5. Debriefing the work of the committee (everyone)

6. Prayer (Frank)

7. Adjournment (The meeting will end promptly
   at 8:30 p.m.)

See attached information

1. Sunday school enrollment trends over the last
   ten years

2. Congregational membership trends, including
   age-specific information

3. Minutes of previous committee meetings and actions
   concerning the Sunday school

We need everyone on board at this discussion to express thoughts and opinions. Bring yourself, your feelings, and your ideas. Talk to others and get their ideas and feelings. Be prepared to share. We are all in this together.

Jane did some new things for the first meeting she chaired. The agenda and supporting documentation were sent out well in advance so that everyone had the same information and time to digest it. Time was set aside before the meeting began so that there would be personal and informal time available to members. Jane planned to arrive at 6:40 p.m. The meeting would begin and end on schedule. She asked Frank to open and close the meeting with a devotion and prayer, asking him to focus on Christ's promised presence and the power and activity of the Holy Spirit. She also asked him to be ready to respond with extemporaneous prayer during the meeting if either of them believed the committee was at a standstill, the conversation was getting too heated, or committee members weren't listening well to one another.

The agenda clearly stated the topic of discussion and the next steps for moving forward. Debriefing was established as part of the process. Jane worked in a business environment in which this process was commonly used, so she knew that people would need to talk about their cognitive and affective responses to the meeting. The premeeting communication delivered encouragement and expectation that attendees come ready to talk. For Jane, there would be no silent members.

Immediately after the opening devotion, Jane addressed the third item on the agenda by saying, "I want us to have an open discussion about the Sunday school. All of you have received background information, including what has been said about this before and what we have agreed to do. However, I do not think we have a clear and comprehensive plan, and I want to go in that direction. But I . . . we . . . need all hands on board. That's what this open discussion is about—ideas, thoughts, fears, suggestions, directions, problems—all of it and all of us. I have asked Peter, our secretary, to keep track of the conversation."

Predictably, Ellery began. He spoke for several minutes and made a couple of suggestions for improving attendance. Jane summarized his comments and thanked him for his contribution. Then there was silence. Jane looked around. She knew that usually after Ellery finished, someone would move to adopt his ideas. Before that could happen this time as well, she said, "We have heard from Ellery. There are five more of us here. I'd like to hear from all of you."

Silence. Eyes downcast. Finally, after what seemed like hours (actually it was only fifty-three seconds), Frank spoke. "I think we have all taken something of a backseat over the last several years. Jane, you are asking us to come to the front seat."

"Yes, I am," she said.

"Okay. I followed your suggestion and asked some others about this, and I have a list of their ideas and some of my own," shared an energized Frank.

When Frank was finished, Jane summarized his comments, checked to see if the secretary recorded his remarks, and thanked him for his contribution.

Georgia spoke next, then Alex, then Peter, then Lucy. Each brought something new. Most also shared what they had heard from others they had talked with before the meeting.

Jane saw that the energy level in the meeting had changed. There were some clear agreements and some clear disagreements as well, but everyone had spoken and half the meeting time was over.

Jane asked Peter to review what he had written, then asked, "What would you say are our next steps?"

Peter spoke first. "I suggest I organize the meeting minutes and get them out to you in the next week. You can then see if I have summarized things as you remembered them. Get back to me with corrections. This has been a wonderful conversation, and I think we need to keep doing this. Everyone has been involved."

Ellery was next. "I could get started with these action items."

"Why don't we wait on that?" Alex said. "We need to talk more so we really do write this next chapter together."

Georgia agreed. So did Lucy, who said, "I think so too. This conversation has been great."

Jane nodded. "Looks like we have a consensus. Peter, we'll see your summary within the week, right?"

"Right."

Jane concluded by saying, "We'll pick up the conversation at the next meeting."

The next item was the debriefing, where everyone was invited to speak. Everyone who spoke was excited and positive, sharing some sense of hope that the committee was getting somewhere.

However, Ellery was silent during the debriefing. Jane noticed this and asked, "You are a key to our work, Ellery. How has this meeting been for you?"

"Different," responded Ellery. "I've heard some things I really don't agree with."

"There are some areas of disagreement. Please, bring those disagreements back to our next meeting," Jane said.

"You bet I will," Ellery snapped.

Where there was compliance and lack of energy before, there was now conflict, questioning, and increased energy. Jane's interventions as the chair of the religious education committee were clear. She set a tone of involvement, which was at times explicit: "We need everyone on board at this discussion and everyone's thoughts and opinions. Bring yourself, your feelings, and your ideas. Talk to others and get their ideas and feelings. Be prepared to share. We are all in this together." At other times, her tone was implicit, as when she sent out useful information far enough in advance that committee members had opportunity to prepare.

Jane used an agenda to establish clear boundaries for the meeting: "The room will be open by 6:45 p.m.; the meeting will begin promptly at 7:00 p.m." She actively and deliberately enlisted the verbal activity and participation of all members of the committee. In order to have a robust conversation, there must be people in the conversation. For a myriad of reasons, though, people may not participate. When this happens, conflict can go underground and participants can then lose passion for what they are doing. The consequence is that they avoid any behavior that may bring conflict to the surface. The goal is to get through the meeting without controversy, so no cutting-edge ideas or controversial items will be discussed. Decisions then become "let's get through this" reactions rather than "let's take a risk" or "let's try a new direction." Jane, by facilitating, fostering, encouraging, and supporting the verbal participation of all members, was encouraging healthy conflict.

As indicated earlier, in a healthy conflict, the concern, problem, or opportunity is known, identified, and spoken about. By acknowledging the conflict, an organization and the people within it focus on clearly defining the issue, mobilizing resources to address it, and focusing on resolution. A major characteristic of this kind of organization is robust collaboration: people come together to express their thoughts, ideas, and strategies concerning the issue. Emotional energy is exerted to solve the problem, embrace the opportunity, and move forward to master the challenge. The focus is on what needs to be faced. Characteristic of this stage is a "we are working together to solve the problem or to engage the challenge" mentality, using a strategy of bringing together people with varying perspectives in order to work toward resolution.

In the literature connected with conflict and its management, there is general agreement that the following attitudes and behaviors are also characteristic of healthy conflict:

1. Everyone values and practices open communication. There are no secrets. Everyone is offered the same information, and discussion is face-to-face. The organization encourages participants to give voice to what is on their mind at the present time while it can be most useful for effective problem-solving. The goal is that everyone says what he or she believes, thinks, questions, or feels about the concern.

2. Everyone seeks clarification rather than assuming that what he or she thinks is fact. Words are a means of interpersonal discourse, but words also have many interpretations and nuances. That is,

what one person means by using a word may not be what another person understands. Confirming meaning is critical.

3. Everyone separates person from problem. This organization focuses on the problem, concern, or opportunity. Someone may say, "We've been friends for a long time, and I expect to continue to be friends with you. That transcends the fact that we disagree pretty strongly on this particular issue."

4. Everyone takes time to work through differences. Sometimes there is pressure to "get this settled," especially when anxiety builds. In healthy conflict, people take the time they need to resolve, as best as they can, the conflict.

5. Everyone focuses on the present and not on past issues or concerns. Old problems do surface because they influence contemporary ones. But healthy conflict does not rework old issues. Past problems are acknowledged, but people are encouraged to work them out in a different arena.

6. Everyone names, faces, and engages problems. Denial and ignoring are kept to a minimum. Acknowledgment of the concern, issue, or opportunity leads to the next step of developing strategies to work on it.

7. Everyone possesses the attitude and belief that conflict is necessary, and its constructive and healthy use permeates organizational life.

In the Christian community, among members of the Body of Christ, there are additional characteristics:

8. Jesus' presence is recognized with thanksgiving, and prayer for the work of the Holy Spirit is constantly made. Jesus promises His presence "where two or three are gathered" (Matthew 18:20). Thus, all gatherings of members of His Body are gatherings where He is present. Those gathered are aware of His presence and give thanks for it. They desire the Holy Spirit's guidance and energy and pray for it. They pray often during meetings, not just as bookends to the meeting.

9. The gift of community is recognized and applauded. The people who join one another in the Body of Christ, even in the midst of conflict, are gifts, present with one another and for one another. Who knows what the Holy Spirit will teach through such gatherings?

Jane's early leadership of the religious education committee focused on naming, identifying, and engaging the problem in as clear a way as possible, using open communication, recognizing the presence of Jesus with thanksgiving, and praying for the work of the Holy Spirit. All characteristics will eventually be in play in her committee, but she chose to set an early tone for dealing with differences and conflicts. Jane believes in full and robust conversation; her leadership reflects that, as does the leadership of all church leaders who want to use differences constructively.

SPEAKING PERSONALLY

I am averse to conflict. There was too much of it as I was growing up, and most of the conflict was never resolved. Often, conflict ended when people were just tired. So it has been hard for me, as an adult, to facilitate conversations that have the potential to bring conflict into the open. Even so, I know it to be absolutely necessary that, as much as possible, everyone has a voice so that what is known to that person (in terms of reactions, feelings, and opinions) is known to others.

As may be clear by now, I appreciate Patrick Lencioni's work. In connection with this chapter, I recommend reading *Death by Meeting: A Leadership Fable*. In it, I found gems like this:

> When a group of intelligent people comes together to talk about issues that matter, it is both natural and productive for disagreement to occur. Resolving those issues is what makes a meeting productive, engaging, even fun. Avoiding issues that merit debate and disagreement not only makes the meetings boring, it guarantees that the issues won't be resolved. And this is a recipe for frustration. Ironically,

that frustration often manifests itself later in the form of unproductive personal conflict, or politics. And so a leader of a meeting must make it a priority to seek out and uncover any important issues about which team members do not agree. And when team members don't want to engage in those discussions, the leader must force them to do so. Even when it makes him or her temporarily unpopular.[58]

I applaud church leaders who intentionally bring together people of differing personality styles and perspectives and then facilitate meetings where everyone has a voice and uses it. Such meetings become energized; creative solutions emerge; people are engaged. I have found that conducting such meetings is not easy. To be honest, I would rather that everyone agrees, ideally with the first suggestion I agree with, so we are quickly done. However, I pray for encouragement, patience, and the capacity to remember that church leaders are called "to equip the saints for the work of ministry, for building up the body of Christ" (Ephesians 4:12). And that means engaging in healthy conflict.

---

58 Lencioni, *Death by Meeting*, 229–30.

CHAPTER FIFTEEN

Warning Signs

> So I find it to be a law that when I want to do right, evil lies close at hand. For I delight in the law of God, in my inner being, but I see in my members another law waging war against the law of my mind and making me captive to the law of sin that dwells in my members. Wretched man that I am! Who will deliver me from this body of death? Thanks be to God through Jesus Christ our Lord! So then, I myself serve the law of God with my mind, but with my flesh I serve the law of sin. (Romans 7:21–25)

By reading this book, you are seeking ways to build up the Body of Christ and fulfill the opportunities that you have to lead. But being a leader in Christ's Church is no easy task and dangers are many. Evil lies close. And I caution you—you will struggle to put the concepts you learn from this book into practice in your life and in your role in your congregation.

Some behavioral signs are real warnings to you; they point to a deterioration of your capacity to effectively lead. What that means is that you are becoming less effective in building up the Body of Christ. You may note that all of the warning signs relate to topics covered in this book, with a few more that are only lightly touched upon. You are in a position to address each warning sign, but your first task is to recognize what is happening.

The list is a difficult one. That is why it is a list of warnings and not of joys. They are warnings to all Christians, even those who are not formally or even informally tasked as church leaders, but they are especially challenging to those who lead. Church leadership brings more demonic attack, and that attack exploits the vulnerabilities of church leaders.

Note that the warnings described in this chapter are all in a state of movement. They are not static. Rather, they are moving in a darker and less healthy direction. Life is not either/or concerning most of the items on this list. Sometimes many of these things occur to a lesser degree, which is bad enough. But when these warnings build momentum, trouble most certainly ensues. So, following is my list of eighteen warnings:

1. You begin to see most of your life and what is happening to you—to your marriage and family, and to your congregation—more and more in secular or "this world" terms. As a result, spiritual resources are used less often: you attend the Divine Service less often, you receive the Eucharist less often, mutual consultation with other members of the Body of Christ is eschewed, prayer is abandoned, Bible study becomes nonexistent.

   These activities are seen as unnecessary to your well-being. You do not recognize that Satan is establishing a foothold, seeking to bring you down as a church leader and as a Christian. You have taken off or are in the process of taking off the lens of spiritual warfare. (If so, review chapters 2 and 3.)

2. You are edgy and increasingly irritable. Conversations often begin with what relationship expert John Gottman calls a "harsh start-up,"[59] which means that there is a strong likelihood that conversations go nowhere (at least nowhere positive). Your blood pressure may be increasing, as is your heart rate. While these physical responses happen from time to time, they are more frequent or even chronic. As a result, your body is deteriorating prematurely.

---

59 Gottman, *The Seven Principles for Making Marriage Work*, 26.

You are short with your spouse and children (if you have them) or your friends. You are functioning at an increased intensity and your creativity and good judgment are decreasing. This is a physiological reality. If so, review chapter 10.

3. You increasingly bring a third party into your conflicts and disagreements. You vent more to others without talking directly to the person with whom you are struggling. This is known as triangulation. What is this? "Triangles serve two purposes: (1) absorbing anxiety, and (2) covering over basic differences and conflicts in an emotional system."[60] Triangles occur whenever a third party is involved, often surreptitiously, in a two-party dispute or conflict.

There was a conflict between Jonah, the chairman of the elders, and another elder, Jamie, concerning some of the changes Jonah wanted to make to the elders' position description. Jamie was especially concerned because, while he really liked being an elder and felt called to be one, he was also working two jobs in support of his wife and three children. Some of the changes Jonah wanted to make would mean that Jamie would spend more time than he had available to serve as an elder. What made this an emotional issue was that Jamie did not think Jonah was particularly empathic to his situation. Whenever he expressed his concern, Jonah countered with a speech about needing to be doing God's will.

By the end of the last elders meeting, Jamie was furious. He ran into another congregation member in the parking lot after the meeting and vented. He did the same with his wife when he got home, in full hearing, he learned later, of two of his three children.

Jamie knowingly created a triangle twice, once with the congregation member in the parking lot and once with his wife. He unknowingly created triangles with two others—his children who overheard him. By the end of his venting, Jamie was feeling better, but by bringing other people into the situation, two intentionally and two unintentionally, he changed the relationship that four

60 Richardson, *Creating a Healthier Church*, 116.

people have with Jonah. Although they have not had direct experience with Jonah, their opinion of him will have changed and they will respond accordingly.

This is a negative triangle. Jamie's anxiety, differences, and frustration were expressed and were felt by the others. George and Natalie in chapter 5 are also examples of negative triangles. Yet not all triangles are negative. For instance, if Jamie had approached Jonah, acknowledged that they were in an emotional dispute, and requested that they meet together with Pastor Joachim to resolve it, both parties would have created a triangle, but it would have been done by bringing in a helpful third person. Be aware when, as a church leader, you increasingly use these triangles in negative ways.

4. You talk much more about people and less to them. This is a direct corollary to warning 3 above. As anxiety in relationships increases, direct conversation tends to decrease. But the anxiety needs a place to go, so it goes to conversations that are about people rather than with them. In some cases, this takes the form of gossip, which is condemned within the Christian community. This response has its roots, however, in the speaker's need to dissipate rising internal tension. If you detect that you are doing more of this, be alert to emotions that are building inside of you and to unhealthy ways they may be expressed.

5. You are doing less listening and more talking. You are abandoning the listening skills you learned. You find yourself hearing some of what other people are saying, but instead of processing their comments, you are thinking of rejoinders. As a result, you and others in the conversation compete for airtime just to make your points. That process simply heightens emotions. Others may be saying, "You aren't hearing me" or "You really don't understand what I am saying" or, even more directly, "You're just not listening." Naturally, you defend yourself, and you hear yourself saying, "Yes I am hearing you, but you are not listening to me." If so, review chapter 6.

6. You are conversing more exclusively with people who agree with you and are distancing yourself from those who disagree. You in-

creasingly read and watch things that support your position. You refuse to listen to ideas, arguments, or opinions from those who disagree, maybe even dismissing them as "ignorant," "biased," or "uninformed." You are certainly holding your ground or position, but you are losing personal connections with those who do not agree with you. You know that listening does not mean agreeing, but you are forgetting that staying connected is equally important. Take it as a warning signal if you are increasingly stating your positions, values, or goals with others who are likely in agreement with you in personal conversation, electronic communication, or other communication channels, yet you are not in an equal amount of conversation with those who differ from you. Echo chambers generally do not produce creative conversations and energized problem-solving directions. See chapters 11 and 12.

7. You are using power more and collegiality less in your relationship with others. When you accept a leadership position, you automatically assume some power. Some examples follow:

> You chair a committee, and you likely facilitate the work of the committee and preside at its meetings.

> You are a DCE, and you supervise minors, over whom you have authority by virtue of your age, experience, and position.

> You are a pastor, and you have the power of the pulpit, which gives you a captive audience, as well as the power of your education and of your office.

> You are a teacher, and you have the power of age, experience, position, and, if in an early elementary grade, most likely physical presence.

Power is misused when you count the votes before you bring something to a committee meeting or voters assembly; when you stand over a seated person while talking to that person; when you regularly arrive late, knowing that the meeting cannot start without you; when you threaten a church worker with financial repercussions. This behavior is based on the capacity for dominance.

Power is necessary, and its use is crucial to the order of things. But the warning here is of its misuse over and against others. As you find yourself resorting to it more and more, you are likely not building up the community. There is even recent research that suggests that the more power a person has, even on a short-term basis, the less neurological activity there is available for that person to be able to experience empathy concerning another person.

Here is another example. When speaking about seminary education (a subject close to my heart), Paul Tripp writes:

> Academized Christianity, which is not constantly connected to the heart and puts its hope in knowledge and skill, can actually make students dangerous. It arms them with powerful knowledge and skills that can make the students think that they are more mature and godly than they actually are. It arms students with weapons of spiritual warfare that if they are not used with humility and grace will harm people they are meant to help.[61]

Here, Tripp suggests that increased biblical and theological knowledge used without connection to what he calls the "heart" is power used in a hurtful way. It is likely true that knowledge is power, and power apart from the empathy and care that comes from a servant heart is problematic. This is not just a concern about clergy; it is a concern about all church leaders, including you and me as well.

As you retreat more and more into an attitude of "I'm in charge" or "You should be doing what I say because I am the chair/church worker/longtime member," consider these behaviors to be warning signs. If so, review Pastor Nathan and Gloria's interaction, as well as Pastor Nathan's interaction with Pastor Francis, in chapter 7.

8. You are seeking information, knowledge, and skills to handle the difficulties you are experiencing in your leadership without first turning to your own assessment and understanding of yourself. Focusing all your attention on changing the other, doing the task,

---

61 Tripp, *Dangerous Calling*, 54.

or fostering the vision or mission without paying attention to your own state is dangerous. You may even be looking for techniques for fixing or changing someone else before taking the proverbial log from your eye. If so, see chapter 9.

9. You are not connecting with people who will help you sort through your situation, style, and feelings concerning your situation. You are becoming increasingly isolated, attempting to handle whatever is going on by yourself. See chapter 2, with special attention to Satan's strategies and the consultation that Jim and Liz had with their pastor.

10. You are experiencing increasing despair, anxiety, depression, or anger. This means that there is more limbic and, perhaps, even more R-Complex activity pressing on your executive functions (the cerebral cortex) to handle. Increasingly, you are acting before thinking. If so, see chapter 10.

11. You know that there are resources offered, including conversation with more experienced colleagues, counseling, and spiritual direction, but you continue to isolate yourself and withdraw, assuming that you should handle the concerns yourself. You find yourself thinking phrases like "If I were a strong-enough Christian, I would be able to manage this by myself" and "I need to work this out on my own because if others saw I was struggling with this, they would not think I was a good leader or even a strong Christian." If so, review the tactics of spiritual warfare in chapters 2 and 3.

12. You are resisting feedback and becoming less transparent. When asked, "How are you doing?" you answer, "Fine," and either keep walking or change the subject. When given the opportunity to debrief at the end of a meeting, you increasingly use distancing language, such as "things are going okay," "we're doing all right," or "it's an interesting time," when things really are not going okay, you are not doing all right, and "interesting" is the word you use when you do not want to say anything else. If so, take a look again at chapter 7.

13. You are becoming increasingly more sedentary, have less restful sleep, and are eating or drinking more without medical reason for doing so. J. H. C. Fritz speaks directly to pastors about this, but his words really apply to all.

> To the spiritual and intellectual fitness of *a pastor* must be added physical fitness, 1 Tim. 5:23. A poor condition of health, a frail body, and a weakened constitution will greatly interfere with the work of a *pastor.* . . . He should therefore give attention to regular habits of life, to diet, sleep, exercise, and recreation. *Mens sana in corpore sano! [Sound mind in a sound body!]*[62]

Your life habits are changing. Conflict is, first of all, a challenge to your health. It has the potential to interfere with your capacity to be a church leader who builds up the Body of Christ. If so, consult with a medical doctor, counselor, or mature Christian colleague.

14. You turn to less healthy ways of handling your stress response. Among these could be television, the Internet, alcohol, and pornography. Additionally, you are becoming more edgy and stressed in other dimensions of your life, meaning that those other dimensions are also going downhill. In the process, you forget the holistic approach to life—that everything is connected. As a result, you begin to compartmentalize more. If so, turn to the next chapter and also consult the second warning on this list.

15. You recognize that the differences you have with others are more intense, and you have a growing sense that you are being attacked and that you are in a competition that you must win. Both your body and your strategic planning build toward the chronic battle in which you see yourself. Others become more and more the enemy. You increasingly seek to recruit others to be on your side of the battle. You are well along in the battle experience when you actively believe that the congregation would be much better off if your adversaries left, or even died. If so, see chapter 12.

---

62 Fritz, *Pastoral Theology*, p. 21, emphasis added.

16. You are less appreciative of others and are increasingly irritated at the way they approach issues during your conversations with them. You are learning to disagree with the German theologian Dietrich Bonhoeffer's assertion that you (and others) should be thankful for the community that is around you:

> Let him who until now has had the privilege of living a common Christian life with other Christians praise God's grace from the bottom of his heart. Let him thank God on his knees and declare: it is grace, nothing but grace, that we are allowed to live in community with Christian brethren.[63]

Whenever anyone suggests that your adversaries might be gifts of the Holy Spirit to you, you grunt and walk away. If so, look again at chapter 11.

17. You are forgetting the strengths that you have and are becoming reactionary. You are forgetting what you know and what your competencies are. Perhaps, though, you are not truly forgetting them; they are just not as accessible to you in this situation. A family educator with the National Alliance on Mental Illness shared with me that she forgot all that she had learned about mental illness when one of her family members began to exhibit symptoms of an illness she had studied. In other words, whatever was known goes out the window under the pressure of the stressors. This is common when stressors mount. If so, see chapter 10.

18. You are increasingly forgetting your Baptism. You continue to sing hymns that celebrate and affirm the sacramental effectiveness of Holy Baptism as you remember your own. But at the same time, you feel farther and farther away from that reality. In that movement away, despite the reality that Christ stays close to you, you forget, or at least do not utilize, your understanding of spiritual warfare. Without necessarily knowing it, you are increasingly caught in Satan's foothold.

---

63 Bonhoeffer, *Life Together*, 20.

Admittedly, this list of warnings is ominous. On the one hand, I want to disturb you. On the other, I want to remind you that most of this list shows natural human emotional and intellectual processes, albeit flawed processes. We are flawed, so our emotional and intellectual processes are imperfect.

However, I want to explain here that there is nothing on this list that I have not experienced myself or experienced when walking with other church leaders. Nothing on this list is pulled from out of thin air. The reality behind these warnings is more common than I want to think about. In some instances, I truly wish I had not experienced them. But one reason I want to tell you that I have in one way or another experienced these situations is to contribute to the Johari Window transparency: I know these warning signs because I have seen them either in my life or in the lives of others. It is likely that you have experienced some of them yourself. Welcome to church leadership. More to the point, welcome to the reality of the Christian experience in this world. Our experience is full of temptation, anxiety, worry, and concern. Martin Luther called this *tentatio*, and he understood it personally and deeply. If we look at our lives, we do too.

Through it all, though, "I am sure that neither death nor life, nor angels nor rulers, nor things present nor things to come, nor powers, nor height nor depth, nor anything else in all creation, will be able to separate us from the love of God in Christ Jesus our Lord" (Romans 8:38–39). Take that, *tentatio*!

Please use this list well. Return to the chapters that address the warnings. Look first not for skills to fix things; look first to Christ. Then, look inwardly at yourself.

Since I ended my warning list with Baptism, I will begin my next chapter there.

CHAPTER SIXTEEN

Good News

Grace to you and peace from God our Father and the Lord
Jesus Christ, who gave Himself for our sins to deliver us
from the present evil age, according to the will of our God
and Father, to whom be the glory forever and ever. Amen.
(Galatians 1:3–5)

I give thanks to my God always for you because of the
grace of God that was given you in Christ Jesus, that in
every way you were enriched in Him in all speech and all
knowledge—even as the testimony about Christ was con-
firmed among you—so that you are not lacking in any
gift, as you wait for the revealing of our Lord Jesus Christ,
who will sustain you to the end, guiltless in the day of
our Lord Jesus Christ. God is faithful, by whom you were
called into the fellowship of His Son, Jesus Christ our Lord.
(1 Corinthians 1:4–9)

We have now walked together along a many-page path. We have covered what I hope is useful territory to you and what is supportive of
your leadership in the Church. I am ending our journey together with
what I believe are attitudes, behaviors, and resources that will continue
to enrich your church leadership and your call to build up the Body of

Christ. Just as there were warnings to you in the previous chapter, here I offer positive direction and support. Church leaders are not only to avoid the negative and evil and bad; they are also to enjoy the positive and beautiful and good. Some of the positive directions and support I include in this chapter call for your active engagement; others are gifts that you receive by God's grace, not by your own doing. All will, I hope, remind you of previous chapters in this book and encourage you to refer to them as you have need. There is also some new material in the list not previously and explicitly discussed in previous chapters.

Like my previous warnings, these are not ranked in order of importance, save the first and the last, which act as bookends. Here are my eighteen pieces of good news for you as you receive and rejoice in God's gifts and as you seek to grow and serve:

1. You increasingly, even daily and hourly, remember your Baptism. In his Small Catechism, Luther writes, "*What benefits does Baptism give?* It works forgiveness of sins, rescues from death and the devil, and gives eternal salvation to all who believe this, as the words and promises of God declare." More than water only, Baptism combines God's Word with the water. It is God's action, not yours. You are God's woman or man because God, in Christ, made it so. In the Lutheran Church, the newly baptized are welcomed using the following declaration:

   In Holy Baptism God the Father has made you a member of His Son, our Lord Jesus Christ, and an heir with us of all the treasures of heaven in the one holy Christian and apostolic Church. We receive you in Jesus' name as our [brother/sister] in Christ, that together we might hear His Word, receive His gifts, and proclaim the praises of Him who called us out of darkness into His marvelous light.[64]

   Simply put, by remembering your Baptism, you are fleeing to Christ and giving thanks for what God has already done for you and for the whole world. This is the very core of your being and

---

64 *LSB*, p. 325.

your identity. You are made one with Christ by God's action, and you are placed into a community that St. Paul calls the Body of Christ.

I encourage you to commit to memory some favorite hymn stanzas that rejoice in this truth so they are always available to you. For instance, consider memorizing the first and third stanzas of "God's Own Child, I Gladly Say It" (*LSB* 594).

You rejoice securely in the fulfillment of God's promises in the birth, death, and resurrection of Jesus, into whose family you have been baptized. As a result, from this center core you are able to see life holistically. This naturally leads to the next point.

2. You see the world and its parts as interrelated and connected. Therefore, you do not create compartments where you delude yourself into believing that one aspect of life does not affect the other. Physical health affects relational health; emotional health affects vocational health; intellectual health affects spiritual health; and so on. Wholeness wheels are a familiar model of the health and wellness movement. You will note two major differences between this wheel (more colorfully developed on the Concordia Plan Services website[65]) and secular wheels. The spiritual component on the secular wheels generally occupies one triangle. In this wheel, Baptism is the axis on which the wheel turns, and spiritual well-being is the surrounding piece that keeps the wheel's components in place. Christ and His work are the core, not just a piece of the wheel.

---

65 "Ministerial Care," Concordia Plan Services of The Lutheran Church—Missouri Synod, accessed July 27, 2015, www.concordiaplans.org/ministry-resources/ministerial-care.HTML.

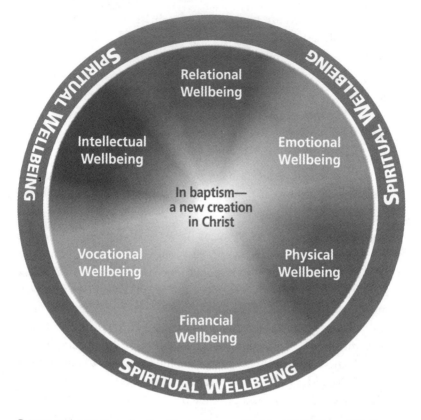

THE WHOLENESS WHEEL

As sanctified children of God, we respond to what God, in Christ Jesus, has done for us by showing proper stewardship of all that we have been given. Among those blessings are the various aspects of our health as shown by the Wholeness Wheel. Our efforts to improve our personal wellness, then, are a part of our sanctified living—as in every aspect "we are to grow up in every way into Him who is the head, into Christ" (Ephesians 4:15). Until that time when we are face to face with God, we strive with His help and guidance to Be Well in all segments of the Wholeness Wheel so we can best Serve Well those in our care.

Spiritual Well-being: Encompassing all aspects of our well-being is acknowledging that our pursuit of wellness is not possible without the righteousness that is ours by grace, through faith in Jesus Christ. It is only through Christ's redeeming sacrifice for us that we seek to nurture our relationship with Him through the study of His Word, prayer, devotion, and worship.

Emotional Well-being: Knowing our full array of human emotions, it is important to recognize which ones are suitable for each circumstance and to express them appropriately. Equally important is striving to respect and honor the feelings of others.

Financial Well-being: Being good stewards in the way we save, spend, and share is crucial to financial well-being. This trait is marked by generosity and eagerness to be a blessing.

Intellectual Well-being: In the same way we exercise our bodies for His service, we continually keep our minds stretched and active by staying curious, asking questions, seeking answers, exploring new responsibilities, and resting our mind at the end of the day to keep it fresh.

Physical Well-being: Honoring our bodies as gifts from God by keeping them as healthy as possible includes nourishing them with healthy food and drink, keeping them fit for service through regular exercise, and respecting our bodies' need for rest.

Relational Well-being: Taking time to nurture our relationships with family, friends, and co-workers through interaction, play, and forgiveness are essential to overall well-being.

Vocational Well-being: In our callings, we carry out our daily work joyfully, serving in the capacity to which He has called us; discovering and using all of the gifts with which He has endowed us; and capably representing Him in the everyday experiences of our vocation, to help Him make this world a better place.[66]

---

66 "Ministerial Care," Concordia Plan Services of The Lutheran Church—Missouri Synod, accessed July 27, 2015, www.concordiaplans.org/ministry-resources/ministerial-care.HTML.

3. You pay attention to your spiritual life. You frequent the Divine Service, participating in the core elements of Confession and Absolution, hearing the Word of God, receiving Holy Communion, and witnessing through word and song to the work and redemption of Jesus. This activity nourishes you. You develop a devotional life, both privately and with others. You regularly discuss your spiritual life with others, and you consult with your pastor (or, if you are a pastor, with another pastor) or a spiritual director.

4. You utilize support systems and intentionally build collegial trust among your peers. You work to develop support networks in all the areas involved in the Wholeness Wheel. You may choose a coach or accountability and prayer partners to develop physical well-being habits and a regular exercise program. You may choose a financial planner to help you and your spouse (if you are married) be as fiscally responsible as possible and save in anticipation of the future. You may initiate regular meetings of people in similar church leadership positions to talk over ways to fulfill your duties and leadership better. You may join a book club or a robust conversational group or join a competitive chess or Sudoku league, for example, to stimulate your intellectual life. You may seek out a counselor from time to time to help you process your emotional responses to your opportunities and challenges. You may seek out a local community college or other continuing education opportunity to enhance your leadership skills. In all cases, you are gathering around yourself diverse people who will help you see things from various perspectives. All of these are simply examples of the principle that you are alert to your support needs and intentional about placing them in your life.

5. You get off the couch or out of the chair, because you know a little exercise goes a long way. You do not need to become a triathlete. You consult with your family doctor, a health educator, your local high school or university athletic department, or fitness coach to develop a plan that fits you. When the plan is developed, you create a support team that holds you accountable and prays for you to accomplish health goals.

6. You actively ask for feedback. You set up mechanisms to achieve this. If you are a salaried church leader, you will ask for an evaluation of your work from the people in the position to do so. For instance, if you are a church schoolteacher, you will ask to be evaluated by your principal and also, perhaps, by your school board. Annual performance reviews are beneficial, but ongoing and frequent evaluations are generally more useful, and recommendations can be implemented a timelier manner. If you are a pastor, you seek direct feedback about your sermons, perhaps utilizing a Monday evening small group gathering for that purpose or creating a DVD of your preaching that can be shown and discussed at your next ministerial gathering.

   If you are a volunteer church leader and chair a committee, you are always building in feedback time at the end of a meeting for members to share their responses to the meeting and to your leadership. As a church leader, you are regularly asking those you serve how they are experiencing your leadership. These are but examples. The point is that you are actively engaged in the feedback process.

7. You actively seek ways and places to be transparent. You are utilizing opportunities for personal sharing and for requesting prayer. You are utilizing more formal sharing opportunities such as consultation, counseling, spiritual conversation—places where you can connect in deeper ways with other members of the Body of Christ. If you chair meetings and open with prayer, you are regularly providing others the opportunity to speak of their own prayer needs (and you will take that opportunity yourself). You trust when appropriate, and you risk saying things that encourage safety for all.

8. You see life as a continuing education opportunity. Thus, your experiences are opportunities to learn and grow. (This fits well with the fourth item of this list.) If you struggle when conducting a meeting, you find a coach who will help you improve in that capacity. If you have difficulty receiving feedback that is intended to be helpful, you find a counselor, mentor, or coach who will help you be more open to feedback. If you have difficulty speaking in public, you join a

Toastmasters event or take advantage of other training opportunities. If you are hijacked by your limbic system, you will develop, aided by a guide, activities that will help you stay calmer. But more than that, you are thirsting for reading and experiences that will aid you in your growth and development. "Be all you can be" is not just a motto for the U.S. Army.

9. You actively monitor, usually with active self-reflection or with the help of a mature colleague, friend, or counselor, influences that affect your participation as a church leader. Some of these influences may be previous experiences; some may be personal stressors that are in your life but not directly related to your church leadership; and some may be influences of your own developmental and growing-up experiences. By being sensitive to these outside influences, you can better discern appropriate concerns for your specific church leadership activities from other concerns in your life, so that you know which is which.

10. You are directly tackling things that you sense are becoming more problematic in your life. Defensiveness goes out the window when there are active dangers to your vocation, your church leadership, or your relationships. You know that getting help may, at first, be difficult or embarrassing. The goal is to deal with the dangers directly. If you feel a depression that casts a dreary cloud over all of your life and makes it hard to accomplish the tasks of your life, much less your church leadership, you will reach out for help! Good Christian counselors are available to you. You will find them, call them, and meet with them!

If you are using alcohol, tobacco, gambling, food, or sex in ways that get in the way of your effectiveness as a person and a church leader—reach out for help! Again, good Christian counselors are around. You will find them, call them, and meet with them. If you are struggling in your marriage (if you are married), in your relationships with the children (if you have children), in your being in the "sandwich" generation of caring for your parents and caring for your children or grandchildren—you will reach out for help.

These are all examples, of course. There is no way I can list all the possible situations that make life problematic. But you get the idea—you are reaching out for help! You are actively developing a support system that will allow you to achieve a healthier lifestyle.

There are many impediments to reaching out, granted. Shame is a major one. There is always the threat of embarrassment, a whole-person experience in which you just want to get away and not be seen by anyone. In response to your shame is God's acceptance of you in and through Christ. This is a love that never ends by God, who sees deeply into you and knows all about you. Likewise, there are people placed around you in the Body of Christ who will likely stick with you through thick and thin, much like a parent who will never quit loving his or her child and who will love you in Christ, regardless. Because you have the promise of the unconditional love of your heavenly Father and there are people in the Body of Christ who are around you, you are never without hope.

11. You increasingly are behaving in trusting and trustworthy ways. When you make a commitment to yourself or to others, you keep it. When you do not, you actively seek to repair the loss of trust by confessing and seeking reconciliation. This honesty of self-disclosure and taking responsibility for what you do aids others in their capacity to trust you, and they are doing so.

12. You seek to enhance interaction with others so they know more about you and so you know more about them. One way you are doing this is that, from time to time, you take yourself out of your comfort zone with the intention of learning more about yourself and others. As an example, you have gone on an international mission trip and have thereby immersed yourself in a different culture. You returned with a different perspective because you discovered things about yourself and your culture about which you were previously unaware.

13. You continue to build your capacity to listen to others and to intentionally seek to better understand them, their ideas and opinions, their feelings and struggles. In doing so, you are gaining a

reputation for being a good listener and, therefore, a person who respects others. At the same time, you are asking others to hear you out so they can understand your ideas and opinions, your feelings and struggles. You know that understanding does not always mean agreement, and you are quite able to take a stand about something important to you without breaking the personal connection with people who differ from you.

14. You are actively protecting opportunities for others to voice their ideas and opinions. As you lead groups of people, you are working to offer hospitality to all voices, remembering that this may bring differences of opinion or conflict. Your goal is quite clear: everyone is heard and respected, even if everyone does not agree with, for instance, a decision or a stand taken.

15. You are talking to people and not about them. Direct conversation is your norm. When you find yourself talking about others, you stop and seek direct conversation.

16. You understand that differences are natural and need to be managed well. You are continuing to increase your skills. You are discussing conflict intensity levels with all of the church leadership so they begin to recognize when conflict is mounting. You are beginning discussions about how conflict is to be handled with your team, your committee, your group, or in whatever context you have leadership influence.

17. You are reviewing the chapters in this book and are beginning to follow up. You may think that some do not apply to you or are not necessary. Perhaps that is true, although I would not have included them if I thought this was so. There is viable research suggesting a gap between a person's acknowledgment of the helpfulness of moving in a healthy direction and actually doing it. You are not just words, but, rather, you are active and intentional.

18. You are remembering your Baptism daily!

Finally, be strong in the Lord and in the strength of His might. Put on the whole armor of God, that you may be able to stand against the schemes of the devil. For we do not wrestle against flesh and blood, but against the rulers, against the authorities, against the cosmic powers over this present darkness, against the spiritual forces of evil in the heavenly places. Therefore take up the whole armor of God, that you may be able to withstand in the evil day, and having done all, to stand firm. Stand therefore, having fastened on the belt of truth, and having put on the breastplate of righteousness, and, as shoes for your feet, having put on the readiness given by the gospel of peace. In all circumstances take up the shield of faith, with which you can extinguish all the flaming darts of the evil one; and take the helmet of salvation, and the sword of the Spirit, which is the word of God. (Ephesians 6:10–17)

All weaponry, all gifts, and all graces are from God, and you are doing your part to use them.

The sacristy prayer often attributed to Martin Luther includes the phrase "Had I been without Your aid and counsel, I surely would have ruined it long ago." This is quite true for us all as church leaders. This is why the beginning and end of this list are embedded in the grace of God in Christ Jesus.

I offer this list to you as manifestations of the message of this book and healthy counterpoints to the warnings listed in chapter 15. We are free to use our gifts, our experiences, our will, and our lives to serve Him. This list provides you ways to think about how you might use your gifts and the opportunities that God gives.

I do not offer the list as a checklist with the notion that if you do them all, you either gain favor with God or are automatically a better church leader. I offer them as behaviors and attitudes that I have found useful for myself and for other church leaders I have talked with. Please use the list—and this book—at the foot of the cross, in the power of the resurrection of Christ, and energized by the Holy Spirit within you!

As We End

As we end our journey together, it is useful to think back on the Bible verses that direct us as church leaders, and from which the title of this book is taken:

> But grace was given to each one of us according to the measure of Christ's gift. . . . And He gave the apostles, the prophets, the evangelists, the shepherds and teachers, to equip the saints for the work of ministry, for building up the body of Christ, until we all attain to the unity of the faith and of the knowledge of the Son of God, to mature manhood, to the measure of the stature of the fullness of Christ, so that we may no longer be children, tossed to and fro by the waves and carried about by every wind of doctrine, by human cunning, by craftiness in deceitful schemes. Rather, speaking the truth in love, we are to grow up in every way into Him who is the head, into Christ, from whom the whole body, joined and held together by every joint with which it is equipped, when each part is working properly, makes the body grow so that it builds itself up in love. (Ephesians 4:7, 11–16)

There is so much in and from the world, in and from our human flesh, and in and from Satan that seeks to destroy relationships in the Body of Christ. I believe that breaking apart relationships is one of the principal strategies of the one who prowls the earth as a roaring lion, Satan himself: attack the church leaders and, in so doing, wound or break relationships in the Body of Christ.

There is an old piece of wisdom that suggests that practically all aspects of good leadership, and certainly church leadership, begin with the establishment of positive relationships. This is because from the very beginning of creation, it was clear that we were not meant to be alone. Psychologist Daniel Goleman writes:

> We are wired to connect. Neuroscience has discovered that our brain's very design makes it sociable, inexorably drawn into an intimate brain-to-brain linkup whenever we engage with another person. That neural bridge lets us affect the brain—and so the body—of everyone we interact with, just as they do us. Even our most routine encounters act as regulators in the brain, priming our emotions, some desirable, others not. . . . During these neural linkups, our brains engage in an emotional tango, a dance of feelings. Our social interactions operate as modulators, something like interpersonal thermostats that continually reset key aspects of our brain functions as they orchestrate our emotions.[67]

As we are not meant to live alone, we are not meant to live apart from a relationship with God. As that relationship with God was healed in the redemptive work of Jesus and brought to us in our Baptism, we now are joined in relationship to others who are similarly baptized and redeemed. Through our Baptism, God deliberately places us into a community. The community receives the newly baptized in these words:

> We receive you in Jesus' name as our [brother(s)/sister(s)] in Christ, that together we might hear His Word, receive His gifts, and proclaim the praises of Him who called us out of darkness into His marvelous light. Amen.

> We welcome you in the name of the Lord.[68]

The community that is a part of the Body of Christ is a gift of God. It is a community of people in relationship with one another. Church

---

67 Goleman, *Social Intelligence*, 4–5.
68 *LSB*, p. 271.

leaders, empowered by the Holy Spirit, lead by fostering and strengthening those relationships. Word and Sacrament are the means God uses to build up individuals in the Body of Christ. Each member of the Body of Christ contributes, and therefore relationships that are joined and sustained by Jesus are vehicles for the building up of the Body of Christ.

Thus, we have walked together to explore how, often from a human relationship perspective, blessed by the Spirit of God, church leaders can lead by using their characteristics, attitudes, and behaviors.

Church leaders take up their roles immersed in a biblical understanding of leadership and church office. They are engaged in spiritual warfare, and they understand the challenges of burnout, stress, and secondary traumatic stress. In other words, they know who they are; they know what their vulnerabilities are; they know what their context is. They know that the major foundation of who they are is that they are baptized daughters and sons of God, made so by the life, death, and resurrection of Jesus, and they live empowered and blessed by God's Holy Spirit.

Church leaders do need to develop certain characteristics and skills: being trustworthy and responsive to others, listening well and deeply, facilitating safe places where people can speak their minds and share the impulses of their hearts. They are people who share openly, solicit feedback regularly, and recognize the multiple influences that shape their capacity to lead. They understand how the brain functions and how environmental factors influence people with different personal styles and ways of doing things. Church leaders deal with conflicts creatively and encourage differences in order to facilitate creative thinking and problem solving.

In so doing, and so blessed by the Holy Spirit, church leaders can, indeed, build up the Body of Christ.

Speaking Personally

My students will recognize at least some of what appears in this book. If they do, it represents a certain amount of consistency on my part. I have shared in this book things that I value and things with which the

Holy Spirit has touched my heart.

I have learned, sometimes painfully, the necessity and value of relationships with others who follow Christ. It has been painful because I learned that value by trying to walk alone, by turning my back on the very community that Jesus has given me. In some ways, writing about the community is a way to remind myself that I am gifted by God to be a member of communities that are a part of the Body of Christ. In that regard, at least it is likely true that I have written first to myself (as self-centered as that might sound), and then to you. Even so, I hope that my writing is useful and helpful, not only to church leaders, but to every reader of this book.

Writing this book allowed me to revisit circumstances and experiences that helped form who I am. No narrative, except where noted, is a direct retelling of a life event. Every other narrative is a fictionalized account of a lived experience that I hope rings true for you, the reader.

Risking another self-serving comment, I want to encourage you to also read *Holding Up the Prophet's Hand*. In many ways, that book and this one very much go together, as I indicated at the beginning. Some information published in *Holding Up the Prophet's Hand* may be helpful to readers of this book.

Finally, the real worth of *Building Up the Body of Christ: Supporting Community Life* is, like church leadership and church offices and positions, in its function and effect.

May the Holy Spirit work to use this book to equip the saints for the work of ministry, for building up the Body of Christ. As church leaders do so, as blessed by the Holy Spirit, they will indeed build up the Body of Christ, growing up in every way into the Head—that is, Jesus. He and His Holy Spirit make the Body grow and hold it together. He and His Holy Spirit make it work properly and increase its strength with the power of love. May Christ do so more and more for the sake of us all, members of His Body.

Bibliography

Aronson, Elliot, Ayala Pines, and Ditsa Kafry. *Burnout: From Tedium to Personal Growth*. New York: Free Press, 1981.

Baab, Lynne M. *Personality Type in Congregations: How to Work with Others More Effectively*. Durham, NC: Alban Institute, 1989.

Blanchard, Ken and Spencer Johnson. *The New One Minute Manager*. New York: William Morrow, 2015.

Bolton, Robert. *People Skills: How to Assert Yourself, Listen to Others, and Resolve Conflicts*. New York: Simon and Schuster, 1979.

Bolton, Robert, and Dorothy Grover Bolton. *People Styles at Work: Making Bad Relationships Good and Good Relationships Better*. New York: AMACOM, 1996.

Bonhoeffer, Dietrich. *Life Together: The Classic Exploration of Christian Community*. New York: Harper One, 2009. First published in English 1954.

Bryce, Nathan K. *Discovering Your Personality Spectrum: Understanding Your Values*. Oren, UT: Insight Learning Foundation, 2009.

Bullard, George W., Jr. *Every Congregation Needs a Little Conflict*. St. Louis: Chalice Press, 2008.

Businessballs. www.businessballs.com

Cameli, Louis J. *The Devil You Don't Know: Recognizing and Resisting Evil in Everyday Life*. Notre Dame, IN: Ave Maria Press, 2011.

Covey, Stephen M. R. *The Speed of Trust: The One Thing That Changes Everything*. New York: Free Press, 2006.

Day, Katie. *Difficult Conversations: Taking Risks, Acting with Integrity*. Durham, NC: Alban Institute, 2001.

Erikson, Erik H. *Identity: Youth and Crisis*. New York: W. W. Norton and Company, 1968.

Figley, Charles R., ed. *Treating Compassion Fatigue*. New York: Brunner-Routledge, 2002.

Fritz, J. H. C. *Pastoral Theology*. St. Louis: Concordia Publishing House, 1932.

Goleman, Daniel. *Social Intelligence: The New Science of Human Relationships*. New York: Bantam Books, 2006.

Gottman, John, and Joan DeClaire. *The Relationship Cure: A 5-Step Guide to Strengthening Your Marriage, Family, and Friendships*. New York: Three Rivers Press, 2001.

Gottman, John, and Nan Silver. *The Seven Principles for Making Marriage Work*. New York: Three Rivers Press, 1999.

Harris, Jeff. "Human Resourcefulness Consulting." Human Resourcefulness Consulting. www.humanresourcefulness.net.

Hartung, Bruce. *Holding Up the Prophet's Hand: Supporting Church Workers*. St. Louis: Concordia Publishing House, 2011.

Heitler, Susan M. *From Conflict to Resolution: Strategies for Diagnosis and Treatment of Distressed Individuals, Couples, and Families*. New York: W. W. Norton and Company, 1990.

Hirsch, John M. *The Process of Reconciliation*. Maitland, FL: Xulon Press, 2012.

Inglis, Holly J. *Sticky Learning: How Neuroscience Supports Teaching That's Remembered*. Minneapolis: Fortress Press, 2014.

Insight Learning Foundation. www.insightlearning.com

Johnston, Gordon. "Old Testament Community and Spiritual Formation," in *Foundations of Spiritual Formation: A Community Approach to Becoming Like Christ*. Edited by Paul Pettit. Grand Rapids: Kregel Publications, 2008.

Kheper, "The Four Humours," www.kheper.net/topics/typology/four_humours. HTML.

Kleinig, John W. *Grace Upon Grace: Spirituality for Today*. St. Louis: Concordia Publishing House, 2008.

Kolb, Deborah M., and Associates. *When Talk Works: Profiles of Mediators*. San Francisco: Jossey-Bass, 1994.

Kolb, Robert, and Theodore J. Hopkins, eds. *Inviting Community*. St. Louis: Concordia Seminary Press, 2013.

Kottler, Jeffrey. *Beyond Blame: A New Way of Resolving Conflicts in Relationships*. San Francisco: Jossey-Bass, 1994.

Lang, Susan M. *Our Community: Dealing with Conflict in Our Congregation*. Minneapolis: Augsburg Fortress, 2002.

Leafgren, Fred, and Joseph Sullivan. *Personality Effectiveness with Style: Facilitator's Workbook*. Addison, TX: Personality Resources, 1999.

Lencioni, Patrick. *Death by Meeting: A Leadership Fable.* San Francisco: Jossey-Bass, 2004.

———. *The Five Dysfunctions of a Team: A Leadership Fable.* San Francisco: Jossey-Bass, 2002.

———. *Overcoming the Five Dysfunctions of a Team: A Field Guide for Leaders, Managers, and Facilitators.* San Francisco: Jossey-Bass, 2005.

Leonard, Sam. *Mediation: The Book: A Step-by-Step Guide for Dispute Resolvers.* Evanston, IL: Evanston Publishing, 1994.

Lott, David B. *Conflict Management in Congregations.* Durham, NC: Alban Institute, 2001.

Ludwig, David. *Renewing the Family Spirit: Overcoming Conflict to Enjoy Stronger Family Ties.* St. Louis: Concordia Publishing House, 1989.

Lutheran Service Book. St. Louis: Concordia Publishing House, 2006.

Marty, Martin E. *Building Cultures of Trust.* Grand Rapids, MI: Eerdmans, 2010.

Melander, Rochelle, and Harold Eppley. *The Spiritual Leader's Guide to Self-Care.* Herndon, VA: The Alban Institute, 2002.

Mind Tools, Ltd. www.mindtools.com.

"Ministerial Care." Concordia Plan Services of The Lutheran Church—Missouri Synod. www.concordiaplans.org/ministry-resources/ministerial-care.HTML.

Murphy, Ed. *The Handbook for Spiritual Warfare*, Revised and Updated. Nashville: Thomas Nelson, 2003.

Nauss, Allen. *Implications of Brain Research for the Church: What It Means for Theology and Ministry.* Minneapolis: Lutheran University Press, 2013.

———, ed. *The Pastor's Brain Manual: A Fascinating Work in Progress.* Minneapolis: Lutheran University Press, 2015.

Nichols, Michael P. *The Lost Art of Listening: How Learning to Listen Can Improve Relationships*, 2nd ed. New York: The Guilford Press, 2009.

Payne, Karl I. *Spiritual Warfare: Christians, Demonization, and Deliverance.* Washington DC: WND Books, 2011.

Pettit, Paul, ed. *Foundations of Spiritual Formation: A Community Approach to Becoming Like Christ.* Grand Rapids, MI: Kregel Publications, 2008.

Putnam, Robert D., and Lewis M. Feldstein. *Better Together: Restoring the American Community.* New York: Simon and Schuster, 2003.

Rendle, Gilbert R. *Behavioral Covenants in Congregations: A Handbook for Honoring Differences*. Durham, NC: Alban Institute, 1999.

Richardson, Ronald W. *Becoming a Healthier Pastor: Family Systems Theory and the Pastor's Own Family*. Minneapolis: Fortress Press, 2004.

———. *Creating a Healthier Church: Family Systems Theory, Leadership, and Congregational Life*. Minneapolis: Fortress Press, 1996.

Ridge Training. www.ridge.com.

Rothschild, Babette. *Help for the Helper: The Psychophysiology of Compassion Fatigue and Vicarious Trauma*. New York: W. W. Norton and Company, 2006.

Saguaro Seminar on Civic Engagement in America. Kennedy School, Harvard University. www.hks.harvard.edu/programs/saguaro

Sampson, Stephen J., and Cindy Elrod. *Applied Social Intelligence: A Skills-Based Primer*. Amherst, MA: HRD Press Inc., 2010.

Sande, Ken. *The Peacemaker: A Biblical Guide to Resolving Personal Conflict*. Grand Rapids, MI: Baker Books, 1997.

Savage, John. *Listening and Caring Skills in Ministry: A Guide for Groups and Leaders*. Nashville: Abingdon Press, 1996.

Sipe, James W., and Don M. Frick. *Seven Pillars of Servant Leadership: Practicing the Wisdom of Leading by Serving*. New York: Paulist Press, 2009.

Sloat, Donald E. *The Dangers of Growing Up in a Christian Home*. Nashville: Thomas Nelson, 1986.

———. *Growing Up Holy and Wholly: Understanding and Hope for Adult Children of Evangelicals*. Brentwood, TN: Wolgemuth and Hyatt, 1990.

Stamm, B. Hudnall, ed. *Secondary Traumatic Stress: Self-Care Issues for Clinicians, Researchers, and Educators*. Baltimore: Sidran Press, 1999.

Steinke, Peter L. *Congregational Leadership in Anxious Times: Being Calm and Courageous No Matter What*. Herndon, VA: The Alban Institute, 2006.

Stephen Ministries. www.stephenministries.org

Tripp, Paul David. *Dangerous Calling: Confronting the Unique Challenges of Pastoral Ministry*. Wheaton, IL: Crossway, 2012

Vaill, Peter B. *Learning As a Way of Being: Strategies for Survival in a World of Permanent White Water*. San Francisco: Jossey-Bass Publishers, 1996.

Walther, C. F. W. *The Proper Distinction Between Law and Gospel*. St. Louis: Concordia Publishing House, 1986.